Investing from a Position of Strength

**Personalize your experience! Enjoy any of six formats in any order.
Go to janiczek.com/strength for links to all.**

READ THE BOOK

The book is designed to be read in an evening or during a short flight. Each of the six chapters explores one core concept, and simple chapter and subsection headings organize key need-to-know aspects of that chapter's core concept.
Estimated time: 1 hour

GET THE PICTURE?

A picture is worth a thousand words, as are the illustrations throughout the book. A quick 15-minute review of these pictures and captions will provide a complete overview of the six core concepts.
Estimated time: 15 minutes

LISTEN UP

The audio recording features a conversation during which the author answers questions about each core concept, elaborating on them in ways that will deepen your understanding. Listen to the audio at janiczek.com/strength.
Estimated time: 2 hours

WATCH THIS

Consider learning or reviewing core concepts by watching a video synopsis. Watch the video at janiczek.com/strength.
Estimated time: 1 hour

WHAT'S MY SCORE?

Use a scorecard to assess your current alignment with core concepts. Then, think ahead one year. What would you like your assessment to look like? Download the scorecard at janiczek.com/strength.
Estimated time: 10 minutes

SHARE IT NOW

Instantly share a digital copy of the book with family, friends and colleagues at no cost! This is a powerful way to demonstrate your commitment to the concepts and begin conversations that can enhance your understanding and results. Go to janiczek.com/strength to share as many digital copies as you'd like, or, if you prefer to send books, you may order them using the same link.
Estimated time: 2 minutes or less

INVESTING FROM A POSITION OF STRENGTH

A high net worth investors guide to thriving in all investment climates

Joseph J. Janiczek

Rankings and/or recognition by unaffiliated rating services and/or publications should not be construed by a client or prospective client as a guarantee that he/she will experience a certain level of results if Janiczek is engaged, or continues to be engaged, to provide investment advisory services, nor should it be construed as a current or past endorsement of Janiczek by any of its clients. Rankings published by magazines, and others, generally base their selections exclusively on information prepared and/or submitted by the recognized adviser. Rankings are generally limited to participating advisers.

Past performance may not be indicative of future results. Different types of investments involve varying degrees of risk. Therefore, it should not be assumed that future performance of any specific investment or investment strategy (including the investments and/or investment strategies recommended and/or undertaken by Janiczek Wealth Management ("Janiczek"), or any non-investment related services, will be profitable, equal any historical performance level(s), be suitable for your portfolio or individual situation, or prove successful. Janiczek is neither a law firm nor accounting firm, and no portion of its services should be construed as legal or accounting advice. Moreover, you should not assume that any discussion or information contained in this document serves as the receipt of, or as a substitute for, personalized investment advice from Janiczek. Please remember that it remains your responsibility to advise Janiczek, in writing, if there are any changes in your personal/financial situation or investment objectives for the purpose of reviewing/evaluating/revising our previous recommendations and/or services, or if you would like to impose, add, or to modify any reasonable restrictions to our investment advisory services. A copy of our current written disclosure Brochure discussing our advisory services and fees is available upon request. The scope of the services to be provided depends upon the needs of the client and the terms of the engagement.

Reviews for Joseph J. Janiczek's books are not, and should not be construed as, an endorsement of the investment advisory services provided by Mr. Janiczek or Janiczek Wealth Management, an SEC registered investment adviser (the "Firm"). No such reviewer is a client of the Firm, and has not commented as to a favorable Janiczek investment experience. Rather, their commentaries relate exclusively to Mr. Janiczek's book.

Award Selection Criteria for Top Financial Advisors. *Barron's Top Advisors:* Rankings are based on data provided by advisors. Included factors were assets under management, regulatory record, revenue produced for the firm, quality of practice and philanthropic work. Investment performance is not an explicit component. *Top Financial Advisors/Financial Times:* Rankings are based on data provided by investment firms. Included factors were assets under management, asset retention, years of experience, FINRA compliance record. Investment performance is not an explicit component. *Advisory HQ:* Rankings are based on data provided by investment firms. Included factors were fiduciary duty, independence, transparency, level of customized service, history of innovation, fee structure, quality of services provided, team excellence and wealth of experience. *Mutual Funds Magazine:* Rankings are based on data provided by investment firms. Included factors were nomination by peers, higher education, professional accreditations, SEC and state registrations, fee structure, assets under management, minimum client portfolio, years of experience and SEC filings. Investment performance is not an explicit component. Worth Magazine: Rankings are based on data provided by investment firms. Included factors were professional designation and background, client retention rates, average portfolio returns, fee structures and sample financial plans were submitted for review. Investment performance is not an explicit component.

Exclusive Signature Series Edition 2018.

Published by Clovercroft Publishing
Franklin, Tennessee
Second Edition
Manufactured in the U.S.A.
Book and Cover Design by Chrysalis Creative Group/Monty Jorgensen

To my dad, for teaching me the importance of strength and how to build it.

TABLE OF CONTENTS

INTRODUCTION

The investment landscape and climate have rapidly changed. How you and the generation before you accumulated, protected and invested wealth over the last 30 years is not likely to be the most prudent way to manage your wealth in the 30 years ahead.

Some long-respected and time-tested strategies are still applicable, like living under your means, diversifying investments, and emphasizing value-priced or small innovative companies. Investing in lean/low cost vehicles and rebalancing portfolios in certain disciplined ways are likely to continue to be solid investment approaches as well.

However, for high net worth investors, those with portfolios in the seven- and eight-figure range, as well as ultra-high net worth investors with portfolios reaching into the nine-figure range, it is an appropriate time to confront new market realities, reflect on past best practices and incorporate select new strategies and innovations. If you presently have a seven- to nine-figure portfolio, you may have acquired your wealth with the aid of the most advantageous market in history from 1982 to 2007, survived the crisis of 2008 and early 2009, and then stayed the course to enjoy a healthy post-crisis rebound still roaring as we go to print with this updated edition. Alternatively, you may have been positioned for a good opportunity post-crisis and have put your relatively new liquid wealth to work in a revived bull market. Still, you may be concerned about what to do as the business cycle matures.

During multi-asset class bull markets, amateurs and pros alike can succeed despite committing a multitude of investment and financial planning mistakes. We've seen wealthy investors with extreme and unadvisable concentrations in commodities, real estate, large cap domestic stocks and even bond portfolios avoid serious portfolio losses despite such positions. We've also seen isolated cases that did not pan out, such as fearful investors remaining nearly 100% in cash during a robust recovery bull market. Regardless of whatever mistakes you got away with (or didn't) or luck you enjoyed (or didn't), it would be foolish not to do your best today to identify and address any and all weaknesses, outdated approaches, or inefficiencies that can hinder your future results.

The investment climate, with the accompanying noise and hype, has become far more challenging, and investors must adapt or risk unhealthy wealth depletion and/or emotional chaos. On the upside, authentic innovations are making it easier to incorporate sound strategies backed by highly credible and respected academic research. Both developments deserve our attention.

The significant changes we are seeing are not likely to be a short-lived aberration. I am an optimist by nature, and I think the future will bring great opportunities and innovations. Nevertheless, I also think it is unwise to assume markets will be so forgiving that you can make fundamental mistakes and still prosper. To thrive in the markets that lie ahead, your best strategy is to assume you need to strengthen your basic approach to wealth management and investing.

I wrote this book to provide you and other high and ultra-high net worth investors with practical solutions to protect and grow your wealth, and allow you to succeed in any investment environment. My hope is that this book will profoundly and permanently transform how you invest and manage your wealth, both in the daunting bear and sideways markets and the opportunistic bull markets that lie ahead.

Enjoy,
Joseph J. Janiczek
February 2018

Chapter One
Why Strength Matters and What It Means

"A financially strong investor is a superior investor."

This observation, distilled from my 30 years in the field of wealth management, is simple and yet so profoundly true, I decided to make it the motto of my company. All too many investors learned this truth the hard way during a major market correction or a financial crisis: You do not become financially strong by achieving superior results; you achieve superior results by becoming financially strong.

Early in life, my family drove home the importance of strength. My family didn't buy the home we lived in, we built it. My brothers and I helped my father pound in the nails that held the frame of the house together, and you can bet we didn't just walk away from boards or joists that still felt rickety. My father built nuclear power plants and oil refineries, structures that must be built to last and able to weather hurricanes and earthquakes. His duties gave him a "stronger is better" way of looking at life, which rubbed off on me.

At just 17, I started my own oil company, and within a few years, I created the first conventional motor oil that could last up to a year between changes. I used chemical additives to boost the properties of conventional motor oil, enabling it to endure extreme temperatures and last much longer than products that had to be changed every three months or 3,000 miles. Companies like Mobil and Castrol released similar products many years later.

While the meaning of strength is obvious in structures and well-built products, the concept of financial strength is often misunderstood. Many people equate it with simple, one-dimensional outcomes, like the value of a portfolio or the total wealth a person has accumulated. While net worth certainly matters, once you get to a certain point it matters less. I have known people with $1 million who were financially strong, and people with $50 million who were not. Strength is not a matter of size; it is a matter of durability versus vulnerability. "Rickety wealth" has not been structured in such a way that it can weather the harshest storms and tremors the marketplace can deliver.

Acquiring Strength

Financial strength resembles physical strength. You cannot accomplish a strong physique overnight. It takes persistent hard work to acquire and discipline to maintain. It is not one-dimensional; you cannot become strong by working one set of muscles and ignoring all the others. It takes insight into which training regimens work and which ones do not. Some people spend hours in the gym with modest results, while others achieve great results in far less time through optimal training. An insightful, experienced coach can work wonders as well.

Likewise, financial strength takes time to acquire, but it is easier to maintain than it is to develop. It is not based on strong performance in one or two areas such as a great salary, or real estate holdings, or strong investment returns. It requires strength in many interrelated areas all across the board.

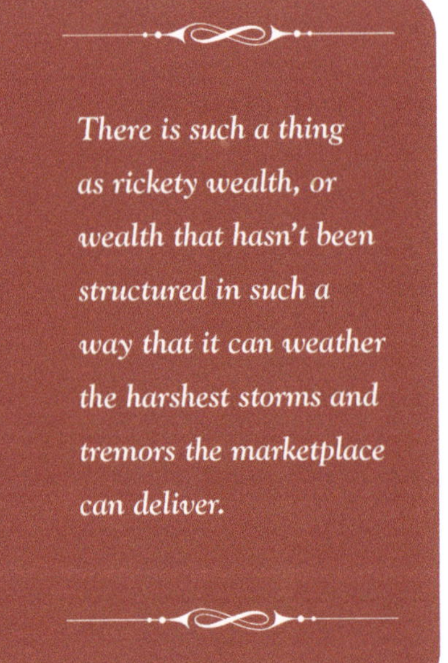

There is one fortunate difference between financial strength and physical strength: If you want a powerful build, you cannot ask someone else to do your exercise for you, but the right financial advisor can handle most of the heavy lifting on your behalf. However, you're unlikely to seek such help if you do not understand what financial strength means. After decades of experience advising clients, I crystallized my strength measurement and building methodologies into the approach known as Strength-Based Wealth Management (SBWM) and integrated it with Evidence-Based Investing (EBI) to tie together the two complementary disciplines (see graphic on page 18). I also was awarded a patent (USPTO #8,903,739) on Systems and Methods for Optimizing Wealth for various unique aspects of the approach. There are many styles of wealth management. However, I find that when I am able to simply and clearly illustrate both strong and weak aspects of clients' finances, they become more engaged and more vividly see actionable areas of improvement and a clear path forward. This is a key benefit of this approach.

I have worked with hundreds of clients over the years, and very few were financially strong when I first met them. Don't get me wrong—these are typically highly accomplished, intelligent people. They have liquid assets

It is not enough to do your best;
you must know what to do,
and then do your best.

W. EDWARDS DEMING

Here is what every high net worth investor needs to do: focus on investing from a position of strength. Do this to the best of your ability and all else will fall in place splendidly.

– Joseph J. Janiczek

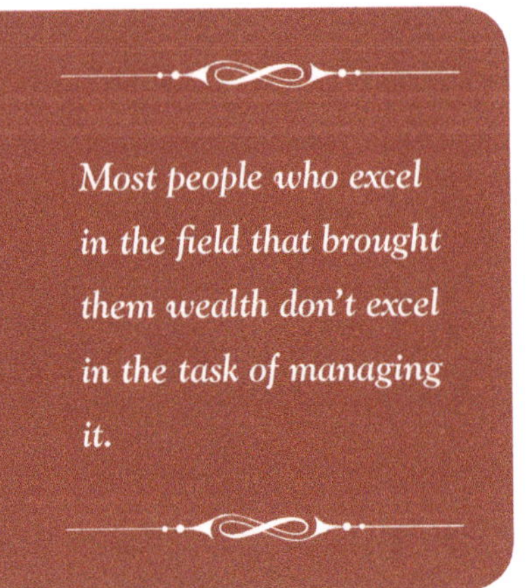

somewhere in the seven- to nine-figure range. A few have had the good fortune to inherit wealth, but most have made their money through sheer hard work and determination. Some are entrepreneurs who built their own businesses, while others have reached high rungs on the corporate ladder. Some have built significant earned income streams in the form of appreciated business assets, and others have turned small stakes into large stakes by good investments in the financial markets or in real estate. Still others have wealth based primarily on a lifetime of prudent saving.

The talent, drive, and good fortune that helps a person acquire wealth doesn't guarantee an aptitude for wealth mastery. In my experience, the two rarely go together. Just as even Michael Jordan could not be great at basketball *and* baseball, most people who excel in the field that brought them wealth do not excel in the task of managing it. There just is not time enough to be great at everything. It is unusual to be introduced to a client who has financial strength to match his or her other strengths. In fact, most people aren't quite sure what I mean when I first use the term "financial strength." I will explain this idea with a story about a gentleman I'll call "Robert."

Robert's Story

When I first met him, Robert was one of the senior-most executives in a large, publicly traded company. From the start, I could see that he was smart and energetic, with a thoughtful, caring side that had made him admired in his company and his community. Thanks to his leadership skills and his strong commitment to his company, he was earning a great income and had accumulated a substantial nest egg. Despite these great advantages and assets that included several nice homes, Robert was not financially strong. He wouldn't have expressed his problem in those words before we met, but he knew he had issues and needed better advice.

Robert realized that he was over-invested in his own company. The industry he was in had the volatility of a game of "Chutes and Ladders," and if his company

"Forgive the mess. Warren just put everything into cash."

fell down a chute, he would take a huge personal hit. But lack of diversification wasn't the only problem he faced. He also lacked clarity. His corporate duties demanded so much of his energy and time that it was hard for Robert to focus on where his investments were and how they were performing. During the booming bull market of the 1980s and '90s, he could all but ignore his portfolio and still achieve good results. As the market hit rough patches, he began to see contraction rather than growth. In the rare free hours available to attend to his personal finances, he found his time consumed by low-value activities, like processing piles of financial mail and paying bills. Instead of seeing and dealing with the big picture, he was slogging through endless necessary but secondary tasks. He recognized that he wasn't managing his wealth anywhere near as well as he was managing his corporate duties.

Robert was getting piecemeal financial advice from several sources, but he didn't have a constructive working relationship with any one advisor. On top of all this, he worried that his wife would be totally lost if anything happened to him and she had to deal with these problems.

There were other cracks in the dike that Robert could not see until I began working with him. He had substantial assets but those assets failed a "stress test." If the market and the economy went in directions they have been known to go in the past, he risked losing much of his wealth, not to mention his lifestyle and his estate. This huge wake-up call inspired him to seek corrective action.

There were smaller problems as well. He had a poorly allocated and ill-managed portfolio, he was paying far more than he needed to pay for transactions, he incorrectly financed his homes, he had totally outgrown his estate plan, and he was not optimizing his stock options. None of these problems was huge viewed in isolation, but accumulated small mistakes, repeated year after year, would have cost him a small fortune in the long run.

Clarity During the Crisis

Some of these problems were fairly easy to solve. Robert didn't realize that there are tools that could help him manage routine financial tasks in a fraction of the time they had previously consumed. He soon learned how much he could save every year by managing his portfolio more efficiently. More importantly, he acquired the system, structure, support, and discipline that are crucial to achieving financial freedom. Gradually, over a period of years, Robert progressed from a patchwork approach to wealth management to a comprehensive approach—one that optimized his assets, estate, and portfolio while protecting his family's lifestyle. In short, he moved from financial vulnerability to financial strength.

This strength was never more needed than in the fall of 2008, when the financial markets underwent their biggest crisis in decades. Many investors panicked, and many fortunes were greatly diminished or even lost. Robert and his family didn't suffer from the crisis. They took advantage of it.

Robert did not panic because he had a clear picture of his assets and overall position. He knew he had the financial strength to weather the sharp global downturn because his portfolio and balance sheet had already acquired the sturdiness needed to pass a rigorous stress test. His wealth and his lifestyle were not in serious danger, and this security allowed him to keep a cool head while others were rattled. I never observed him in a state of doubt, he operated, from my perspective, in a state of excellent financial control.

Because he possessed a broad understanding of financial strength, he knew that problems in one area, like tumbling stock and real estate prices, created opportunities in other areas, like estate planning and distressed real estate investing. While many investors compounded the crisis by making bad decisions, Robert in my opinion, made sound decisions. Thanks to clarity, confidence, and the long-term bargains a crisis creates, he came out of this challenging situation stronger than he went into it.

There's a lot more to Robert's story than his outstanding financial performance. Like nearly all the people who have worked with my company, Robert sees wealth as a means to an end, not an end in itself. For Robert and his family, the goal is a happy, well-balanced life. Career success often comes at a very high cost to other essential pursuits and desires—time with family, adventures and hobbies, helping others, your faith, or lifelong learning. The value of financial freedom is not measured in dollars. It is measured by the ability to devote yourself to the things that give your life meaning. On top of attaining robust financial strength, this is Robert's most meaningful achievement. He has not left the business world entirely, but he has given work its proper place in the hierarchy of his life's priorities.

While some details of this account have been changed in respect for "Robert's" privacy, the main thrust of his story is accurate. It reflects, in part, the benefits of achieving financial strength, and I say "in part" because there are other advantages. A strong investor is a superior investor, but he or she is also a superior negotiator, a superior executive or leader, a superior entrepreneur, a superior benefactor, and a superior role model in his or her family, social circles, and community. Strengths engender confidence, and confidence will enhance your performance at any major task you seek to accomplish.

If Robert had stayed on the path he was on when I met him, he might have lost a tremendous amount of his wealth in the 2008-09 financial crisis. Today, he might be doing what so many investors are doing—licking their wounds and nervously navigating the market with greater effort but less confidence and security.

You cannot control the ups and downs of the market, but you can pursue financial strength that allows you to thrive in virtually any market. It is not something you can accomplish overnight; the time required depends on your starting point. Once you attain a position of strength, you can move from sporadic and inconsistent results to consistent and calculated results. You can master wealth and achieve real financial freedom.

In sharing Robert's story, I cited four essential attributes—system, structure, support, and discipline. These essential attributes are so vital to financial strength. Think of them as the "Four Pillars of Strong Investing." Let's examine what happens when investors lack these attributes.

FORMULA FOR SUCCESS: SBWM + EBI = WEALTH MASTERY

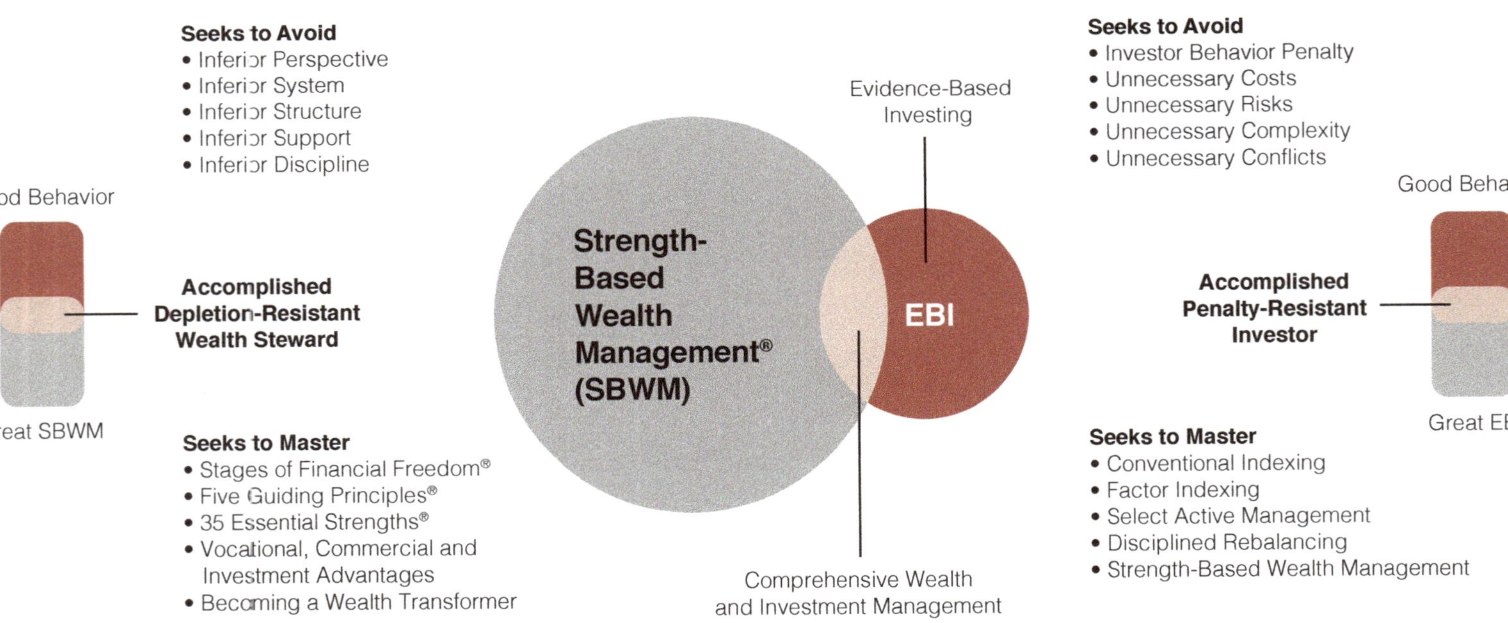

Seeks to Avoid
- Inferior Perspective
- Inferior System
- Inferior Structure
- Inferior Support
- Inferior Discipline

Seeks to Master
- Stages of Financial Freedom®
- Five Guiding Principles®
- 35 Essential Strengths®
- Vocational, Commercial and Investment Advantages
- Becoming a Wealth Transformer

Seeks to Avoid
- Investor Behavior Penalty
- Unnecessary Costs
- Unnecessary Risks
- Unnecessary Complexity
- Unnecessary Conflicts

Seeks to Master
- Conventional Indexing
- Factor Indexing
- Select Active Management
- Disciplined Rebalancing
- Strength-Based Wealth Management

Chapter Two

Typical Investors, Typical Mistakes

In 1929 Winston Churchill, the future British Prime Minister, was touring the United States and Canada. Churchill had just stepped down as Chancellor of the Exchequer, a high government post equivalent to the Treasury Secretary in the U.S. Freed from his duty of overseeing financial policy for the British Empire, Churchill had time to focus on his personal wealth management. In a letter to his wife, Clementine, dated September 19, he boasted of his success in this new pursuit:

> *Now my darling, I must tell you that very great & extraordinary good fortune has attended me lately in finances. Sir Harry McGowan asked me—rather earnestly—before I sailed whether he might, if an opportunity came, buy shares on my account without previous consultation. I replied that I could always find 2 or 3,000 £ [British pounds]. I meant this as an investment limit, i.e., buying the shares outright. He evidently took it as the limit to which I was prepared to go in a speculative purchase on margin. Thus he operated on about ten times my usual scale ... So here we have really recovered in a few weeks a small fortune ... This 'mass of manoeuvre' is of utmost importance and must not be frittered away.**

About six weeks later on October 29—a day known as Black Tuesday—, Churchill was in New York City watching the market drop 12% on the heels of a 13% drop the previous day. He dined that night at the house of the great financier Bernard Baruch, who had invited 40 of the city's top bankers to meet Churchill. Recalling the dinner later, Sir Winston wrote that "... when one of them proposed my health, he addressed the company as 'friends and former millionaires.'" †

Churchill's small fortune wasn't "frittered away," it was decimated. The losses were more devastating because he had been purchasing stock on margin. It took him many years to crawl out of the financial hole he found himself in.

* From Winston and Clementine: the personal letters of the Churchills, edited by their daughter, Mary Soames. New York: Houghton Mifflin Harcourt, 2001

† From Churchill and America by Sir Martin Gilbert. New York: Free Press, 2005

The market had peaked two weeks before he wrote the optimistic letter quoted above, and didn't surpass its 1929 apex until November, 1954.

It is hard to think of a modern public figure more accomplished than Winston Churchill. He was a tenacious leader, an orator without equal, an adept military strategist, a great writer honored with the Nobel Prize in literature, and a talented painter. When it came to money, however, Churchill was not a towering figure; he was average. He was a typical investor who made typical mistakes. He struggled constantly to maintain his lifestyle. He didn't write for pleasure; it was his income. For all the other great strengths he possessed, he was not financially strong.

Part of Churchill's difficulty with money was self-inflicted; he agreed to follow dubious, highly risky investment advice. I see people making the same mistake today and for much the same reason. Churchill fell into a trap that well-known author Jim Collins calls the "undisciplined pursuit of more." For reasons that were partly due to manufactured need, and partly due to the frenzy of his time, he made decisions based on his wants, not prudence or discipline. In striving for peak returns, he took risks that left him dependent on earned income. I have seen investors do the same thing more recently, abandoning a steady, balanced approach to wealth mastery and investment discipline to pursue leveraged hedge funds, unbalanced portfolios, unsustainable spending rates, crypto-currency during its wild west days, and a host of pricing bubbles.

An exceptional quarter century comes to a close

In matters of money, Churchill was also unlucky: Bear markets were more the rule than the exception for much of his adult life. Today, investors in mid-career or nearing retirement age have had an entirely different formative experience. Most have prospered in what I would term a secular, multi-asset, mega-bull market*.

The 25-year period from 1982 to 2007 was arguably the single best quarter century ever enjoyed by U.S. investors. Bonds were in a bull market that extended throughout this whole period. Stocks were in a secular (long-term) bull market from 1982 to 2000. There was one memorable decline in 1987, when the market suffered its largest one-day drop in history (22.6 percent). But that "Black Monday" proved to be a mere hiccup in the Dow's climb from a value of just over 800 in 1982 to 11,722 in January 2000.

multi-asset, mega-bull market: a multi-year period of above average returns in several asset classes primarily at the same time. In the U.S., 1982 to 2007 had bonds, stocks, and real estate performing in this manner.

Look at market fluctuations as your friend rather than your enemy; profit from folly rather than participate in it.

WARREN BUFFETT

Investing from a position of strength helps give you the fortitude and resources to invest at opportune times—when others are too afraid or too broke to do so—and to sell when others will pay hefty premiums. This position of strength includes the superior ability to ride out market storms and the superior maturity to leave some upside on the table.

– Joseph J. Janiczek

As the year 2000 unfolded, we entered a secular bear market*, but the overall bearishness of stocks was tamed for the next seven years by a trio of factors.

- Bonds remained a strong haven for any diversified portfolio.
- While stocks remained in a deep slump from 2001 to 2003, real estate continued to rise. Property values stayed strong through 2007, bolstering the net worth and peace of mind of many investors.
- Stocks enjoyed a cyclical (short-term) bull market from 2003 to 2007, topping 14,000 before their precipitous drops in 2008 and 2009.

Then in March 2009 through 2017 (as we go to press with this updated edition), bonds, real estate, and equities (mostly U.S. large cap stocks) continued a strong recovery bull market.

A multi-asset, mega-bull market is wonderful in terms of the wealth it creates, but it also has a capacity to generate false assumptions and bad habits. Some people still assume the unusual quarter century before 2007 was normal, and the nine+ year slow recovery after the crisis is the new norm. It was not! Just as the Great Depression was extraordinarily bad, a 25-year multi-asset, mega-bull market is exceptionally good. We are not likely to see such extended good fortune repeated anytime soon. We may not see it again in our lifetimes for reasons I'll explore at the end of this chapter. In any event, simply waiting for exceptionally good times to roll again is not a sound strategy. You are better off preparing for all conditions.

You're better off preparing for all conditions, from storms and droughts to beautiful, sunny spells.

Unfortunately, the extended summer we exited recently gave rise to habits that aren't well suited to harsh or volatile climates. The most common bad habit I come across is neglect. A prolonged bull market is like canoeing downstream; it does not take much effort or great advice to get where you're going. You can all but ignore your portfolio for long stretches and still do quite well. You can have an advisor who gets his ideas from the media, not from careful, systematic analysis. You can pay transaction costs and fees that are unnecessarily high and not notice. In short, you can drop your guard and nonetheless be rewarded, not walloped. Bull markets can cover a multitude of common investment mistakes.

secular bear market: a multi-year period of negative real returns in stocks. In the U.S., 1906-21, 1929-42, 1966-82, and 2000-? are great examples of secular bear markets.

The Investor Behavior Penalty

However, there is one mistake that even a long bull market cannot offset, and you will be astonished to hear just how common this mistake is. I was surprised when I first saw research that quantified the "Investor Behavior Penalty."

There is a common assumption that average market performance and average investor performance are roughly synonymous. If the market has a good five-year run, investors have a good run. If the market is down over five years, investors, on average, lose money. However, since the market almost always goes up in the long run, a patient and diversified investor should get solid long-term results, right? That is what most believe.

The problem is that investors, on average, do not succeed in taking advantage of long-term trends.* They do not approach the market in an entirely rational, wholly prudent way. Great market news excites people and spurs them to buy when prices are high. Sharp drops and prolonged downturns discourage or frighten people into pulling back and liquidating assets.

I have seen this happen many times. Nearly every new client has made this mistake. They maximized their deposits into accounts during up times, and minimized their holdings just as values were set to start a cyclical run-up. My Aunt Sophie was a Depression-era woman who never bought stock because she could still remember people who lost everything in the 1930s. In August 1987, after five years of watching stocks rise steadily, she finally decided she was missing out on a good thing and wanted to jump into the market—right at one of its peaks. Fortunately, I delayed her decision long enough for her to avoid Black Monday, which came one month later. On the other side of the ledger, I've seen people crushed emotionally in bear markets. They say, "I just can't take it anymore!" and they liquidate everything—just in time to miss the next huge rebound. On reflection, it seems that every time the market peaks or hits bottom, I get a call from someone eager to buy or sell at the worst possible moment.

You can see this phenomenon on a macro scale. In 2000, the year the mega-bull market in equities finally ended, investors poured more than $200 billion in new money into stocks—the highest infusion of new cash ever. They were boarding a train that had already run out of steam. The market yo-yoed all that year and wound up down 3 percent. The next two years were much rougher. By the fall of 2002, the market was filled with undervalued stocks and poised for the four-year cyclical bull market* that followed. But investors put less than $40 billion in new money into equities that year. They got off the train, just as it was ready for another very good run.

You can see the long-term consequences of rear-view mirror investing in a study by Dalbar Inc., a leading financial services market research firm. The

cyclical bull market: a rally within a secular bear market that is significant enough to make above average returns if an investor is disciplined enough to reduce equity exposure prior to secular risks once again putting pressure on stock prices. The 2003-2007 cyclical bull market is a great recent example.

Dalbar study* looked at month-by-month data that showed when investors bought shares in mutual funds, sold those shares, or exchanged them for other shares over a 20-year period (1989 to 2008). All this data on investment decisions allowed them to simulate the behavior of an "average investor." Here's what they found.

- Over the 20 years studied, the S&P 500 had average returns of 8.4% annually.
- The inflation rate over this timeframe was 2.9% annually.
- The average mutual fund investor had returns of 1.9% annually.

That's right. The average investor didn't keep pace with inflation. Investors actually did fairly well in 14 of the 20 years studied, but the bad decisions they made in the other years significantly undermined their long-term performance. Dalbar stated its own conclusion succinctly: "When the going gets tough, investors panic." This investor behavior penalty has been identified in many other studies as well with differing but all significant behavior penalties identified (see illustration below).

Investor Behavior & The Impact on Investment Performance

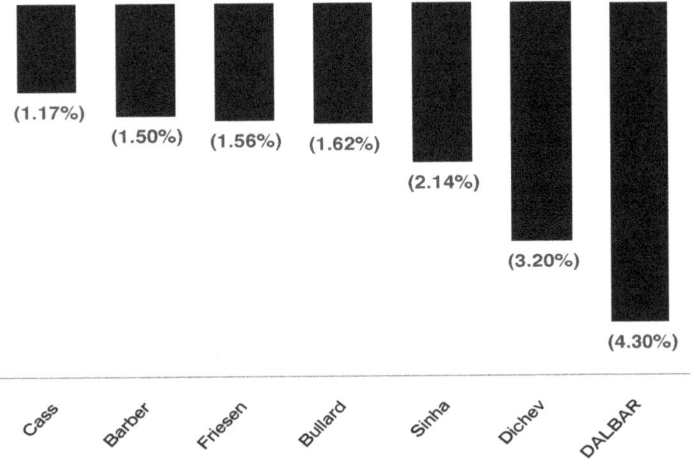

Source: The Laws of Wealth by Daniel Crosby, 2016

Each Study cited uses different periods of time, which can certainly account for differences in amounts. More importantly, the aim of this reference is to show how they all illustrate a material reduction in return attributable to investor behavior.

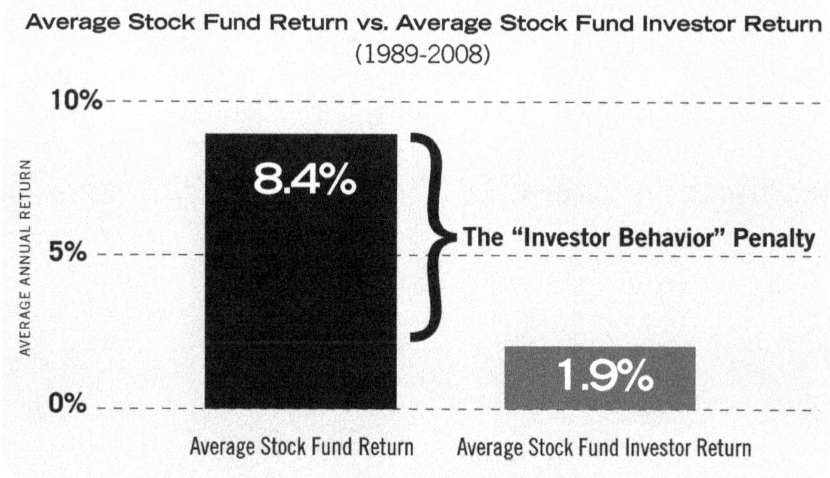

Source: "Quantitative Analysis of Investor Behavior, 2009," DALBAR, Inc. www.dalbar.com

The media's role in inspiring "crazy behavior"

Benjamin Graham, the man who taught Warren Buffett how to invest, has advice that is frequently quoted but routinely ignored: "Individuals who cannot master their emotions are ill-suited to profit from the investment process." Buffett decided to leave New York City precisely because he found that the city wasn't helping him to think clearly. He explained his return to his hometown of Omaha this way:

"I used to feel when I worked back in New York, that there were more stimuli just hitting me all the time, and if you've got the normal amount of adrenaline, you start responding to them. It may lead to crazy behavior after a while. It is easier to think here."†

These days, even if you're far removed from the fray of Wall Street, it takes discipline to avoid the clamor emanating from the financial media. While some of the available commentary and advice has value, many outlets prefer speculation, drama, and trendiness to facts and sober analysis. There is a tendency to fixate on the ups and downs of industries and companies, and to make investing seem more like a sporting event than a patient, deliberate, thoughtful process. To borrow from an old phrase about newspaper editors, many financial news outlets divide the wheat from the chaff, and see that the chaff is published. The self-defeating investor behavior observed in the Dalbar study is often the product of a media-driven stampede.

* Investors Find No Shelter. Dalbar press release, 3/9/09. http://www.dalbar.com/Portals/dalbar/cache/News/PressReleases/PressReleases20090309.pdf

† L. J. Davis. "Buffettt Takes Stock." New York Times Magazine, April 1, 1990. Accessed at http://www.nytimes.com/1990/04/01/magazine/buffet-takes-stock.html?ref=warren_e_buffett&pagewanted=7

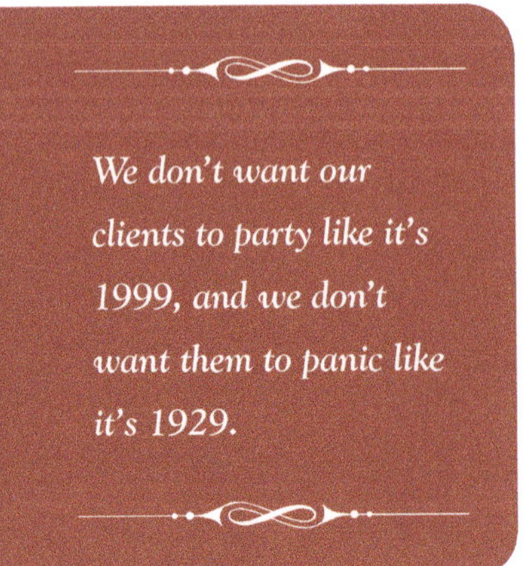

For example, before the brunt of the financial crisis hit in 2008, the S&P 500 was hovering near 1,300. We had some major concerns and allocated most portfolios to 15% to 20% under neutral equity positions with the proceeds from stock sales going to cash. By the end of the year, the index had plummeted to 900, and continued its slide until it fell below 700 in March 2009. At the time, "experts" proclaimed that the bad times were likely to last indefinitely. Some warned of runaway inflation, while others predicted a new Great Depression.

That was possible, but it seemed quite unlikely to me and the other professionals at my company. The media amplified fears based on shallow analysis; we looked at more timely and sophisticated analyses of market values and economic indicators.

On March 5, 2009, we issued an alert to clients estimating that there was just a 5% chance of a depression going forward, and a 30% chance of choppy markets (fluctuations with no real progress in either direction). On the positive side, we saw a 50% chance of a cyclical bull market, with the S&P rebounding to between 950 and 1250. We estimated there was a 15% chance that this rebound would mark the beginning of a secular bull market. Our basic message was, "This is not the time to surrender and liquidate your holdings." In fact, the S&P bottomed out on March 9, just two business days after our alert, and was back to 1,115 at the end of 2009.

Similarly, in April 2010, we identified that stock prices were getting frothy and identified a 77% chance of a 10% or more decline. Our aim was to keep clients from getting overly aggressive. Within 90 days, a sell-off occurred and trimmed 13%± off the top, giving us the opportunity to make further portfolio adjustments at better valuations than in April. This is the art of navigating choppy markets with disciplined rebalancing strategies, a skill best mastered from a position of strength.

One of the principle duties of a quality investment advisor is to temper emotional swings and caution against excessive pessimism or optimism. We do not want our clients to party like it is 1999, and we don't want them to panic like it is 1929! We want them to approach investing proactively, not reactively. Once you achieve a position of strength, it is much easier to be proactive.

Innovation vs. entitlements

With the multi-asset, mega-bull market receding into the past, financial strength is more essential than ever. There are reasons to be quite positive about what the future holds, but also growing reasons for concern. The result could be very choppy market conditions.

On the down side, the investment landscape has fundamentally changed in ways that could hinder future market performance. The exploding level of government debt is a worldwide problem. At the very least, it generates increased pressure for higher taxes, which would lessen the money available for purchasing, productivity gains, and investments. At worst, it raises the specter of a future financial crisis akin to the crisis that struck Greece in 2010. The rapid increase in debt is pushing America into uncharted waters, and it is hard to predict what perils we might encounter.

The aging of our population is also, in economic terms, a depressant. On average, people reach their peak spending level in their mid-40s, and most Baby Boomers are now past that age. Looking at these factors plus other indicators, they suggest that future conditions will be more challenging than the markets many investors have grown accustomed to.

"I've learned to live without a lot of things, Herb, but money isn't one of them."

creative destruction: "process of industrial mutation…that incessantly revolutionizes the economic structure from within, incessantly destroying the old one, incessantly creating a new one. This process of Creative Destruction is the essential fact about capitalism. It is what capitalism consists in and what every capitalist concern has got to live in."
Joseph A. Schumpeter "Creative Destruction" From Capitalism, Socialism and Democracy (New York: Harper, 1975) [orig. pub. 1942], pp. 82-85

On the positive side, we should never underestimate the power of innovation, and applied innovation is the primary engine of wealth creation. Consider the snowball effect of the microchip on economic growth. Advances in microprocessor speed and capacity have spawned new industries and transformed old ones. In the prosperous 25 years I described above, we saw the birth or coming of age of PCs, software, cell phones, and the Internet. We saw the tech revolution remake manufacturing, home entertainment, retail marketing, and the media. In 2007, who could have foreseen today's flourishing iPhone "apps" industry? These are changes that Baby Boomers could scarcely imagine when they were young, and the next generation is poised to bring innovations of similar magnitude and impact. We cannot predict what form they will take or when they will arrive, but we know incredible innovation will happen, and strong investors will nurture its growth and profit from it. That's why I view the future optimistically. While some issues temper my outlook, I believe innovation will win out in the longer run.

There is a saying that there is no such thing as bad weather, only inappropriate clothing. Likewise, clothing yourself in financial strength can reduce your exposure dramatically during bad investment seasons.

In fact, investing from a position of strength will allow you to weather downturns and seize the tremendous opportunities they create. It will put you in a position to buy when others are too fearful or unable to take advantage of values. In good times, strong investors know how to maximize opportunities, with a discipline that protects them from over-optimism. This is the balance strength provides.

Chapter Three

The First Pillar: System

One Good System Trumps 100 Good Actions

Henry Ford is recognized as the father of the auto industry, largely on the strength of one innovation: the automotive assembly line. Looking back at the process he pioneered, Ford recalled the inefficiencies it replaced:

> *A Ford car contains about five thousand parts. ... In our first assembling, we simply started to put a car together at a spot on the floor, and workmen brought to it the parts as they were needed in exactly the same way one builds a house. ... The rapid press of production made it necessary to devise plans of production that would avoid having workers falling over one another.* ***The undirected worker spends more of his time walking about for materials and tools than he does in working; he gets small pay because pedestrianism is not a highly paid line.**** *[Emphasis added]*

Ford knew that in his new system, the assembly line, there were high-value tasks, such as welding the parts of a car together, and there were tasks with little or no value, such as fetching tools and parts. The more workers were occupied by the former tasks and not the latter ones, the more efficient the overall system became.

The same principle applies to investing, which is why I consider a good system to be the first pillar of financial strength. Strong investors focus on tasks that have the most impact. They understand the difference between a low-value activity, like day trading stocks, and a high-value activity, like strategically identifying and moving funds into asset classes that are undervalued. They know there is a world of difference between activity and progress, and they avoid tasks that create the illusion of progress while providing scant results.

By contrast, most investors who strive to actively manage their assets often do so in a haphazard or ad hoc manner. They might have good decision-making skills, but these skills are wasted by looking at various issues in isolation. They do not see their assets, tangible and intangible, as an interconnected whole—

* From My Life and Work by Henry Ford. New York: Doubleday, Page & Company, 1923

as a system, in which the function of one component always affects some other component. It is impossible to make a system operate more efficiently if you fail to see the connections, or worse, fail to recognize that you're dealing with a system. Such failures lead inevitably to a problem I call the 85% Trap.

The Essential 15% Versus the 85% Trap

The 85% Trap is derived from the work of W. Edwards Deming, whose ideas helped to revolutionize the way industries engineer quality into products. Deming observed that 85% of the problems that businesses encounter are due to the systems and processes put in place by management. Just 15% of problems could be traced to mistakes made by workers.

Consequently, if we want to improve the quality of a product or service offering, we need to focus on the system, not on isolated actions. Conversely, if we assume the system is fine and focus solely on actions, we can waste enormous time and expense and have very little to show for it.

Unfortunately, this mistake is very common in wealth management. Investors typically put 85% of their effort into activities that influence just 15% of their results. That's what I mean by the 85% Trap.

There is a simple reason that most investors fall into this trap: They do not follow a systematic approach to wealth management, so they have no system to optimize, just an endless series of one-off decisions and actions. They might understand the value of a good system in theory, and they might use one in their business or professional pursuits, but they do not have the time or knowledge to apply this crucial concept to their finances. This is a huge mistake—the flaw at the root of all other problems.

Investors who lack a system tend to get absorbed by secondary activities. "Robert," the gentleman I discussed in Chapter 1, spent a lot of time sifting through mail and paying bills. Other investors devote large chunks of time staying abreast of financial news. They learn a great deal about individual companies or industries, or the ups and downs of overseas markets. There is nothing inherently wrong with increasing knowledge, but there is something wrong in imagining that knowledge alone will insure success. As Warren Buffett put it, "If past history was all there was to the game, the richest people would be librarians."

Investors who are stuck in the 85% Trap have an "outside-in" view of success. They behave as though the key to mastering wealth is "out there somewhere," and the challenge lies in finding that key and putting it to

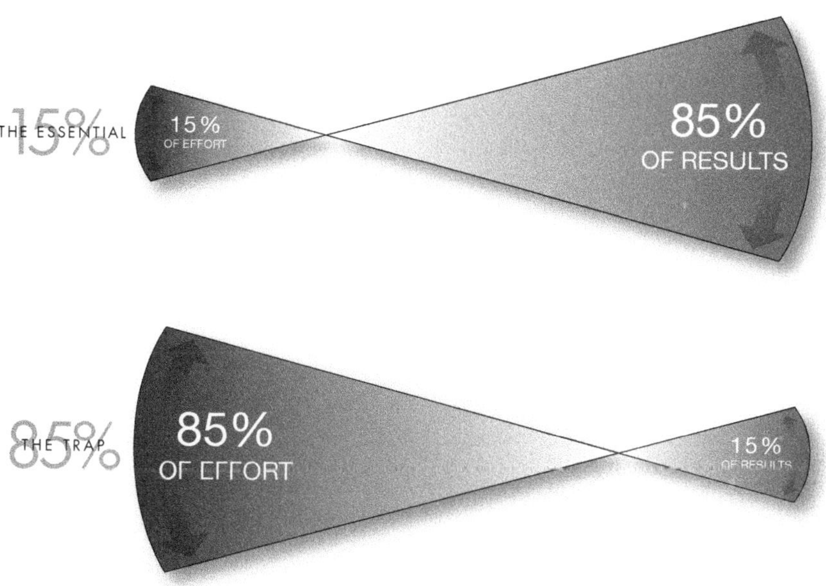

good use. Tangled in complexity, they end up being reactive, undisciplined, and inflexible. Many high net worth investors are stuck either attempting to manage their portfolios on a part-time basis with amateur tools or with financial service representatives who may have impressive credentials but lack the system and expertise to avoid the 85% Trap.

One of the critical steps in mastering wealth is to escape the 85% Trap by focusing on what I call the Essential 15%. Do not waste 85% of your effort on activities that influence only 15% of your results. Focus instead on the 15% of wealth management activities that lead to 85% of your success.

The best investors recognize that success in any endeavor starts on the inside and then moves outward. To master wealth, begin by investing in yourself. Your habits, attitudes, talents, and support system have a much larger impact on your long-term success than anything that lies outside your control. Ensuring you have a good system for crafting plans and making financial and life decisions is an excellent place to start.

Principle for Devising a Robust System

Henry Ford's solution to paying workers for time spent "walking about" was a new system, the assembly line, an idea he adapted from the overhead trolleys used in the meat processing industry. "The first step forward in assembly came when we began taking the work to the men instead of the men to the work," Ford later wrote. That slight but critical shift in thinking led to a huge leap in productivity. Average production times for a car fell from 21 days to 9 hours. The price of a Ford-made automobile fell from $950 in 1909 to $355 in 1921.*

Like any successful system, Ford's assembly line was designed around guiding principles.

- Each worker would have one task and one task alone.
- The line itself had to be "man high" so that workers would not waste time and get fatigued by constant stooping.
- The speed of the line was calibrated to ensure that a worker was neither rushed nor left biding his time. "He must have every second necessary," Ford wrote, "but not a single unnecessary second."

A system for managing wealth also needs a clear set of guiding principles. Through refinements over the years, I've managed to trim my own set of principles down to five:

1. Make your balance sheet, cash flow, and portfolio your friend.
2. Compare your finances to standards of excellence and utilize them to direct you to making optimal enhancements.
3. Stress-test your plan under various scenarios to further reveal strengths, weaknesses, and possibilities.
4. Know what is pulling you forward, holding you back, and serving you best—essentials to having optimal energy, confidence, and focus supporting your plan.
5. Be specific and proactive by identifying and implementing the actions that will result in the best permanent changes.

It is worth taking some time to look at what each of these principles means in practice—the benefits of observing them and the risks of ignoring them.

1. Make your balance sheet, cash flow, and portfolio your friend, not your foe.

There is a critical distinction between possessing a high net worth and having a strong balance sheet, cash flow, and portfolio. Problems in these three areas can give rise to huge frustrations and mistakes. The predicament of a gentleman I'll call "Harry" illustrates this point.

*Ford, My Life and Work

In terms of net worth, Harry was in an excellent position, with total assets valued at somewhere north of $60 million. I would have thought it safe to assume that his balance sheet, cash flow, and portfolio were spectacular, but that was not the case. A very high percentage of his assets was locked up in a private company he owned, or in his homes and other personal property. In fact, when I first met him, his liquid and semi-liquid assets were not sufficient to sustain his rate of spending for much longer. Though he had a $3 million portfolio, he was beginning to tap it at an unsustainable rate. Harry was wealthy and he felt wealthy, but he was heading toward an inevitable cash crunch.

Part of Harry's problem was that he needed to be more cost conscious. A lot of his cash flow problems came down to over-paying for various goods and services. His mortgage payments were much higher than they needed to be. He was bleeding cash in the form of high brokerage fees. He was paying far too much for financial advice and services that were focusing on the 85% Trap and missing the Essential 15%.

Harry's predicament showed how balance sheet problems can cause a domino effect. Because so much of his wealth was locked up in assets that generated expenses but no income, Harry felt that he needed to compensate for this problem through high-risk investments. If he had more control over his cash flow, he would not have felt so much pressure to pursue higher returns. But as it was, the strategy he was pursuing had a fatal flaw. If his high-risk investments suffered a sharp decline, the hole he was in would grow very deep in a hurry. His cash flow would have plunged below the level he needed to meet his financial commitments.

When that happens—when your cash flow becomes your enemy, not your friend—you find yourself forced to raise cash by selling assets you would much

"Well, gentlemen, there's your problem."

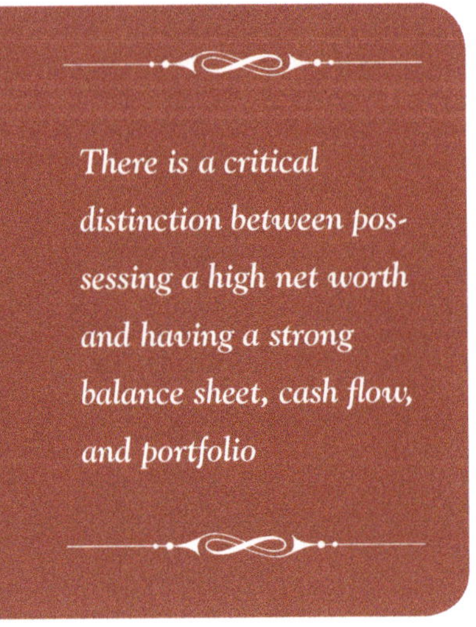

rather keep. This pressure can come at the worst of times, when assets are temporarily undervalued at distressed levels.

Even if that is not the case and you can still squeeze by, you may find yourself handcuffed and unable to take advantage of opportunities that arise in a distressed market. One of Warren Buffett's most quoted recommendations is to "be fearful when others are greedy and be greedy when others are fearful." But you can't be "greedy" (I prefer the term opportunistic) unless you've learned unless you've learned to make your balance sheet, cash flow, and portfolio your friend. If you gain the financial strength such friendship provides, you will be well positioned to acquire the undervalued investments that abound in the depths of a bear market.

This principle raises a question: How do you know if your balance sheet, cash flow, and portfolio are your friend? What standard should investors use to measure the "friendliness" of their current position? The answer lies in the second guiding principle.

2. Compare your finances to standards of excellence and utilize them to direct you to making optimal enhancements.

When people with wealth describe to me how they view their current position, they use a wide variety of yardsticks to measure themselves. Some are troubled because they are comparing themselves to friends, family, or associates who appear to be much better off. Others are troubled because they have lost a large portion of their net worth through market declines, bad investments, or business setbacks.

It is more common, though, to meet people who feel quite confident and secure because they're doing much better than they imagined they would when they were younger. Their confidence may be fueled by the good opinion of others around them, since wealthy, successful people are often accorded tremendous respect and kid-glove treatment.

There is nothing wrong with these benefits of success, but you can't allow them to lull you into false assumptions about your financial position. If you want to know where you really stand in terms of financial strength, you need to employ objective standards of excellence.

Much of the research I've conducted over the past quarter century has been aimed at discerning the standards that top investors use to evaluate their position. How much liquidity should you maintain in bank accounts or other accessible holdings? What levels of semi-liquid and retirement assets need to be accumulated to maintain your standard of living? What attributes are most consistent with the best-performing portfolios? What attributes do the best balance sheets have in common?

There is a correct answer, or a narrow range of correct answers, for all of these questions and 100 others besides. Because of my personal duties as a fee-only, fiduciary* advisor, I've made it my business to determine best practices in all of these areas. As an investor, you do not need to duplicate this research, but you do need to make sure you are working with someone who uses standards of excellence, not guesstimates. And you need to use these standards to assess your own position and decisions objectively.

One group of essential standards involves the long-term durability of wealth. How do you know if your wealth is solid or rickety—susceptible to collapse in an acute or prolonged downturn? That brings me to my third guiding principle.

3. Back-test and stress-test your plan under various scenarios to further reveal strengths, weaknesses, and possibilities.

The "Elastic Limit" is a term I've borrowed from engineering because it has tremendous relevance in wealth management. It refers to the amount of stress a material can withstand before undergoing permanent deformation. For example, if you stand on a wooden bench, the wood may sag a bit and bounce back when you jump off. However, if several NFL linemen stand on the same bench, the wood will probably warp, crack, or break.

In wealth management terms, the elastic limit is the stress your balance sheet can absorb before becoming irreparably damaged. It is not simply a function of net worth. A well-built $2 million financial plan can fare much better in the long run than a poorly constructed $20 million plan.

Too many financial advisors all but ignore worst-case scenarios in their planning. They use average market performance to project your situation in the future, assuming, for example, that inflation will stay at 3% to 4% annually, and market returns will conform to their historic 8% average. But life does not

fiduciary: In a fiduciary relationship, one must act at all times for the sole benefit and interests of another, with loyalty to those interests.

conform to the law of averages. If it did, all American families would have 1.86 children.

Other advisors are somewhat more sophisticated. They calculate long-term risk by employing a Monte Carlo analysis*, which can generate thousands of scenarios. The resulting report can look very comprehensive and impressive, but there's a problem. The analysis almost always excludes the extreme ends of the bell curve. If you ran a typical Monte Carlo analysis of weather on the Gulf Coast, it would have shown the risk of hurricanes, but excluded both Camille (a catastrophic Category 5 hurricane in August 1969) and Katrina (a Category 3 hurricane in August 2005 that proved to be one of the two deadliest hurricanes and the costliest hurricane in the history of the United States).

The best way to stress-test a portfolio is to look at what markets have done historically, and assume that what has happened before might very well happen again. My own team uses actual market and inflation data going back to 1900 (earlier data is not considered reliable). This data set allows us to analyze any financial plan and portfolio and determine how well it would have fared in the best, the median, and the worst financial climates, all viewed in terms of 40-year increments. If the plan's elastic limit is not strong enough to withstand worst-case scenarios, it can be reinforced in ways that don't significantly reduce the plan's performance in favorable market cycles. The goal is to achieve at least a 95% likelihood that the plan is "Depression-proof," and, if possible, to design a plan that has a zero percent probability of depletion. That's one more concrete example of "financial strength."

4. Know what is pulling you forward, holding you back, and serving you best. This is essential to having optimal energy, confidence, and focus supporting your plan.

Wealth mastery can't be pursued without a degree of self-mastery and self-knowledge. You need to know what is working against you and deal with it. You need to know what you have in your favor and use it to the best possible advantage.

In my experience, people often lack such self-awareness, which is why I have made it one of my guiding principles to take proper time for reflection. With weaknesses especially—habits of mind that can hold you back—people often need a third party or a sympathetic ear to surface issues.

Monte Carlo analysis: A mathematical means of analyzing complex instruments, portfolios and investments by simulating the various sources of uncertainty affecting their value, and then determining their average value over the range of resultant outcomes.

I've met people who have allowed a setback to scar them in some way. One gentleman lost a job and assumed he was too old to be of interest to other companies. He was letting his experience and talent go to waste instead of pursuing other professional opportunities for which he was clearly qualified. I've known people who allowed market setbacks to leave them too risk averse or too eager for risk. The former are reluctant to return to the market at all, and they risk missing out on wonderful opportunities. The latter feel like they have to resort to a high-stakes gamble to earn back the wealth they've lost.

Other people I've met were held back by complexity. They've accumulated so many different accounts in so many places, they could fill a bathtub with the financial reports they receive each quarter. Other people are held back from prudent planning by overconfidence. They assume the money they're making now will always be available, and they want to live a lifestyle that could leave them broke if they lost their current position. One role of a quality advisor is helping clients see themselves clearly and not get sidetracked by anxieties, false assumptions, distractions, or unreasonable expectations.

Sometimes, it is harder to help people find their real passions than it is to point out problems. Problems are often more obvious to outsiders, while passions hide and must be coaxed to the surface. Many successful people have a hard time articulating what they really want most in life because they have so many opportunities to choose from. They have family commitments and business responsibilities, plus they serve on boards, assist charities, attend to portfolios and properties, and participate in wonderful leisure activities. When so many things compete for your attention, it is easy to become scattered, if not downright paralyzed. You may overlook or under-pursue the things that matter most to you.

It is critical to know what excites you most, because mastering wealth becomes a pointless and uninspiring exercise if your wealth is not directed to some purpose—to a "WHY?" Finding that "WHY" is not a "touchy-feely" exercise, but a necessary strategy. It is one of the most essential components of the Essential 15%, and one of my most enjoyable roles as an advisor.

5. Be specific and proactive by implementing the strategic actions that will result in the best permanent changes and advantages going forward.

Over the years, I have had the privilege of observing how clients meet challenges and tackle opportunities. Some have a knack for succeeding in any task they take on, while others seem to struggle more than they need to. Eventually, I saw a key distinction between these two groups: Successful people are usually very specific and proactive, while those who struggle tend to be vague and reactive. They set goals, but they do not follow through with a plan of specific actions aimed at meeting those goals. Consequently, instead of controlling events, they wind up responding to events. Getting stuck in reactive mode is another example of the 85% Trap.

By contrast, when successful people see a need or set a goal for themselves, they develop a specific plan of action. In keeping with the concept of the Essential 15%, they strive to find a permanent solution to every challenge, as opposed to a solution that requires ongoing effort.

Let's look at a common goal, saving money, as an example. People who are vague and reactive might set this goal, but their "plan" for increasing their savings could be as fuzzy as "Try to keep an eye on spending." A "solution" like this demands a constant renewal of resolve, and this resolution can vanish in response to unplanned events or mood swings. It is much more effective to say, "I will change the amount of my income transferred directly into my savings and investment plan from 10% to 15% each paycheck." That is a specific, proactive, long-term solution.

Sometimes, a good permanent solution is as simple as engaging the right talent to help you manage ongoing needs like accounting and estate planning. Other times, the solution is knowing what you should stop doing in order to do something else that's more valuable in the long-term. For example, you might decide that your career would benefit greatly by volunteer service on a national industry board or advisory group. A person who is vague and reactive might say, "That's a great idea, but I just don't have the time." A specific, proactive person says, "I'll make the time by retiring from another board, or delegating one or two of my projects." Any task that has the advantages of the Essential 15% is worth doing, and you'll have time to attend to such tasks if you avoid the 85% Trap.

These are simple examples, but you can apply this basic approach to any type of goal. You start with the end in mind by asking, "What is my desired outcome?" For each objective identified, ask, "What is a specific, proactive, and, if possible, permanent solution?" This is how successful people march forward through life. They do not try to solve the same problems over and over again. They devise permanent solutions that give them the freedom to pursue new challenges and growth opportunities.

These five guiding principles provide a powerful and systematic approach to making important decisions, focusing on what matters most, evaluating options, and building financial strength. The key to success lies in using them consistently, not haphazardly.

Make everything as simple as possible, but no simpler.

ALBERT EINSTEIN

Five Guiding Principles, 35 Essential Strengths and the system, structure, support and discipline to master them—a concrete, proven method to make wealth management "as simple as possible, but no simpler."

– Joseph J. Janiczek

To achieve the desired consistency, I find that people need a well-designed structure, something a good advisor ought to provide. Structure is the second pillar of strong investing, and in the next chapter, I will explain what it looks like and why it is essential.

Chapter Four

The Second Pillar: Structure

The Right Assets in the Right Order

Charles Koch is CEO of Koch Industries, Inc., which employs 70,000 people in 60 countries and had $100 billion in revenues in 2008. Koch Industries is a private company, the second largest in the world just behind Cargill. Charles took the helm of the family-owned business in 1967, and he has steadfastly refused to cash in on his 42 percent stake by taking the company public. He wants to preserve his freedom to manage the company in accordance with his principles, and no one can argue with the enormous success of his approach. A $1,000 investment in Koch Industries in 1960 would be worth $2.3 million today. That's a growth rate more than 30 times higher than the S&P 500 during the same period!*

Charlie says, "It is often more difficult to overcome success than adversity." To avoid the perils success often brings, he developed a structure called Market-Based Management (MBM) that helps his companies continually learn and grow at an accelerated rate. There are five very simple components to MBM: Vision, Virtue and Talents, Knowledge Processes, Decision Rights, and Incentives.

Koch Industries is a conglomerate, a vast and far-flung enterprise that includes oil refining and chemicals, minerals and fertilizers, polymers and fibers, pollution and process controls, commodities trading, ranching, and consumer products. Many public companies shy away from this level of product diversification because conventional wisdom deems it "unmanageable." But Charlie and his team don't merely manage all this complexity; they do it with stunning results thanks to Market-Based Management. MBM is a structure for success. It provides order and simplifies complexity by pinpointing the most essential tasks on which Charlie and his leadership team need to focus. The better they get at refining and mastering this structure, the more successful Koch Industries becomes. You can learn all about this in Charlie's book, *The Science of Success* (Wiley).

* "Since 1960, the value of the Standard & Poor's 500 grew about 73-fold, assuming the reinvestment of dividends. During that same period, the value of Koch Industries grew nearly 2,400-fold, using the same assumptions." http://charleskoch.com, 06/30/10. Overview

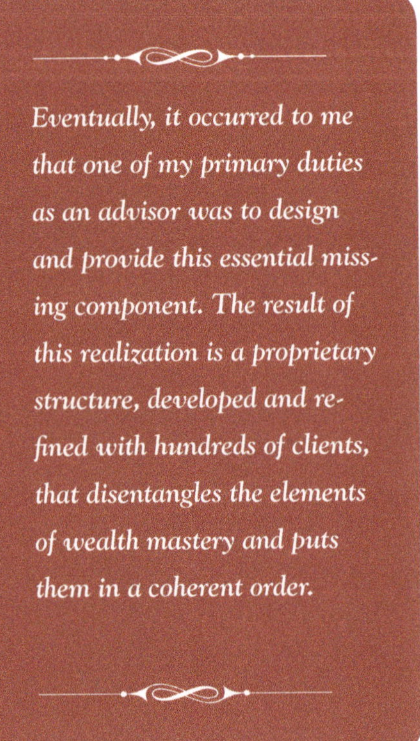

Structure is the second pillar of financial strength. The value and utility of structure are all around us. I do not mean just the physical realm—buildings and roads, the electrical grid, computers and the Internet, etc. I also mean the relationships and organizations that form our personal networks. A company is a structure, as is a team, a school, a family, a church, and a community. And when structures of any size and type have all the right people and pieces working together, they provide an environment that allows us to thrive.

Given how much we rely on forms of structure elsewhere in our lives, one would think most investors would readily grasp this idea and apply it vigorously. Strangely enough, most investors or advisors I meet have not taken this step on their own.

As I've said, the people I advise are very successful. They all have portfolios in the seven- and eight-figure range. I know that clients who live in this space are much better at accumulating wealth than they are at managing it. When it comes to wealth accumulation, they have a business or professional structure that facilitates success. But when they approach wealth management, they lack structure and the great benefits it brings.

A quality structure has these characteristics:

1. Enhanced clarity and awareness. Structure provides order, order provides clarity, and clarity provides awareness and focus. The right structure reveals what's in the right place and what's missing. It highlights interdependencies among different parts of the whole, and it makes it easy to track the consequences of every action.
2. A sense of direction. The clarity that structure provides tells you where intervention is needed. Threats and opportunities stand out clearly, making it much easier to set priorities and make decisions.

3. Confidence. Ambiguity leads to anxiety, but seeing where you want to be and how to get there builds confidence. Understanding your strengths positions you to exploit them; understanding your weaknesses positions you to address them. Both result in increased confidence.
4. Consistency and control. A structure that consists of Essential 15% elements equips you to influence results at the highest level of leverage. Operating at this level enables consistency and control.
5. Superior results. Clarity, confidence, and control add up to great performance and results. You may not outperform the S&P 500 by a factor of 30, as Charles Koch has done with his MBM structure, but you're almost sure to exceed the results of typical investors who lack a structure.
6. Automated success. The right structure makes it easy to succeed. You do not need effort and muscle to make it work. Success becomes routine, because it prompts you to act instead of you prompting it.

How would you like to have a wealth management structure that delivers these six advantages to you? Do you think your investment results would improve and your wealth would grow if you had this structure in place?

It occurred to me that one of my primary duties as an advisor was to design and provide this essential missing component. The result is a proprietary structure, developed and refined with hundreds of clients, that disentangles the elements of wealth mastery and puts them in a coherent order. When clients get their first look at the structure, they are often blown away by its simplicity.

35 Essential Strengths

In the following bonus material, you'll find an overview of my comprehensive wealth management structure. Within the example Wealth Optimization Plan for High Net Worth Investors, you'll see a key feature of the plan called the 35 Essential Strengths, a key component of my patented Strength-Based Wealth Management (SBWM) methods.

Though there may be other valid ways to delineate and arrange financial strength, my experience suggests these are the 35 attributes that top investors get right. Together, they provide a framework investors can use to gauge their position objectively, because each of these 35 strengths is based on well-researched standards of excellence.

When I work with clients, I analyze their financial position in depth, then I show them how they stack up against these objective standards. The model is color-coded—green for strong, yellow for issues, and red for big issues. At a glance, new and longtime clients, whether financially sophisticated or not, can see where they are strong, where they are slightly weak, and where they have a serious vulnerability.

Consequently, this structure shows precisely where action is needed, and it helps define solutions that won't detract from any other essential strength. It helps you escape the 85% Trap and focus on the Essential 15%. Furthermore, it provides a structure for ongoing wealth optimization. You can see where you are gaining strength and whether you are losing ground. The structure tracks and incites progress.

When most people first see this structure applied to their financial position, they are invariably confronted with a fairly substantial amount of yellow and red. Considering the success these people enjoy, and the fact that they are within the top 1% of the country in terms of their net worth, you might think they would be discouraged to learn they have so many issues to resolve. Yet, I have not seen one client respond negatively. Typically, they are relieved to have clarity, to know where they stand, and what they must do to strengthen their position. This clarity creates focus and a sense of urgency. It also creates an all-important alignment between spouses. I have observed that the universal language of green, yellow, and red color coding enables financially sophisticated and unsophisticated spouses to get on the same page and focus on the same issues. This helps matters greatly.

Some of the 35 Essential Strengths are relatively easy to gain, while some are more challenging and take longer to attain. The good news is you don't need to be in Warren Buffett's league to achieve all these strengths. I firmly believe that any investor with a portfolio of $1 million or more can acquire all 35 strengths and maintain them. Once you reach this threshold, you have the critical mass and resiliency of wealth you will need to optimally invest from a position of strength.

When I go through my initial analysis with new clients, I find that, on average, a typical high net worth investor has a dozen or so of the strengths in place. From time to time, I encounter a person who has worked so hard and had such a great sense of direction that he or she arrives at my door with 20 or more strengths already nailed. But this is quite rare.

No matter your starting point, it does not take a long time to make meaningful progress. People beginning with 12 strengths often improve to 24 or more strengths within six months. It depends on where you are starting

BONUS MATERIAL

WEALTH OPTIMIZATION PLAN™
for
HIGH NET WORTH INVESTORS

What does a plan to continually build and maintain an ultimate level of financial strength look like? What does an automated system and structure for analyzing, measuring and reporting strengths, weaknesses and vulnerabilities look like?

In this six-page folio, I provide an example of a Wealth Optimization Plan™ for high net worth investors. This plan includes the Five Guiding Principles™, 35 Essential Strengths™ and an intuitive Wealth Optimization Dashboard™ designed to provide sophisticated and unsophisticated investors alike with a precise overview of their strengths, weaknesses and vulnerabilities. For information on a service that provides the system, structure, support and discipline needed to master this process, see About Janiczek Wealth Management on pages 82-84.

FIVE GUIDING PRINCIPLES

1. Make your balance sheet, cash flow and portfolio your friend not your foe.
2. Compare your finances to standards of excellence and utilize them to direct you to making optimal enhancements.
3. Back-test and stress-test your plan under various scenarios to further reveal strengths, weaknesses, and possibilities.
4. Know what is pulling you forward, holding you back, and serving you best – essentials to having optimal energy, confidence, and focus supporting your plan.
5. Be specific and proactive by identifying and implementing the strategic actions that will result in the best permanent changes and advantages going forward.

THIS BONUS MATERIAL IS PROVIDED COURTESY OF:

Wealth Optimization Dashboard™ Example

Following is an example of how Janiczek Wealth Management proprietary technology reports the results of an analysis of each client's finances in all thirty-five areas.

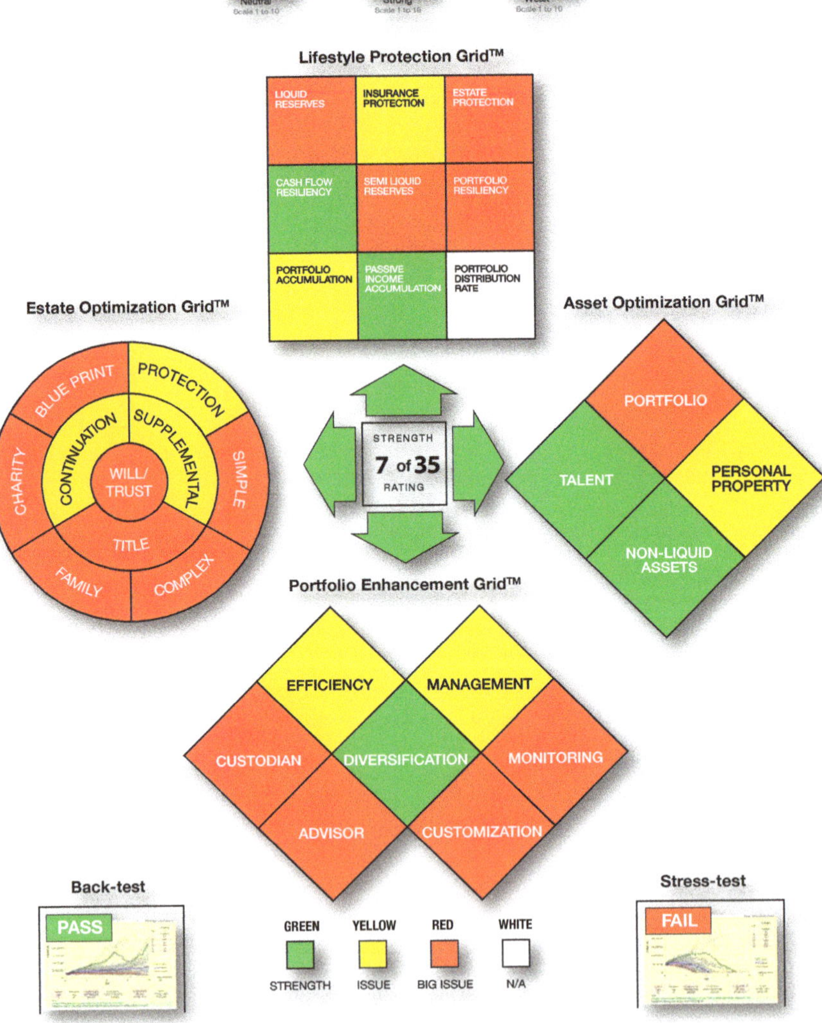

The Fundamentals (3 Strengths)

Balance Sheet

- Having a strong balance sheet with all weaknesses or vulnerabilities eliminated or mitigated.

Cash Flow

- Living comfortably under your means with cushion, surplus, awareness and control consistently serving you.

Portfolio

- Having a well allocated and performing investment portfolio generating current income and long term capital appreciation commensurate with your circumstances, objectives, risk temperament and time horizon.

Lifestyle Protection (9 Strengths)

Liquidity

- Having an optimal level of liquid reserves—no less, no more.

Insurance

- Having an optimal level of insurance coverages—no less, no more.

Estate Plan

- Having proper estate plan documents available at a moments notice to optimally serve you and your loved ones.

Semi-liquid

- Having an optimal level of unencumbered fixed income and equity securities.

Cash Flow Resiliency

- Having relatively low levels of fixed expense obligations such that your outflow is easily sustainable, even in crisis conditions.

Portfolio Resiliency

- Having optimal portfolio risk/reward characteristics matched to your needs and circumstances, and the prevailing investment climate.

Portfolio Accumulation

- Having accumulated an optimal level of semi-liquid and retirement portfolio assets in proportion to your standard of living and predictable passive income sources.

Passive Income

- Having an ideal level of predictable passive income sources in proportion to your standard of living.

Portfolio Distribution Rate

- Having a portfolio distribution rate that is sustainable even during extended bear markets.

Asset Optimization (4 Strengths)

Portfolio

- Having an optimally structured and managed investment portfolio void of costly penalties, complexities and inefficiencies.

Talent

- Putting your endless energy, interest and ability and others' optimally to work to create wealth, multiply results and better manage time.

Personal Property

- Having the optimal level of personal assets enhancing your lifestyle, yet void of harming your balance sheet or cash flow.

Non-Liquid Assets

- Having an optimal level of high performing business and/or real estate assets generating high levels of current income and long-term capital appreciation.

Portfolio Optimization (7 Strengths)

Advisor

- Having a fiduciary, fee-only, full breadth lead advisor that provides the structure, system, support and discipline necessary for long-term portfolio management success.

Custodian

- Having investment accounts consolidated at a safe, efficient, unbiased, and robust custodian.

Efficiency

- Having optimal cost efficiency as an advantage in your portfolio management.

Diversification

- Having an optimal level of portfolio diversification—no less, no more.

Management

- Having an optimal level of value added portfolio management, talent, and systems serving you.

Monitoring

- Having a consolidated monitoring system that provides you with performance, allocation and tax clarity.

Customization

- Having your portfolio optimally customized to your needs and circumstances, on an ongoing basis.

Estate Optimization (10 Strengths)

Will/Trust

- Having well prepared wills and trusts optimally customized to you, your current circumstances and current laws.

Title

- Having optimal ownership and beneficiary elections that are coordinated with your overall estate plan.

Supplemental

- Supplementing your wills and trusts with other useful legal documents that serve you and your family in the event of disability, incapacitation or death.

Protection

- Having optimal asset protection and family lifestyle protection, commensurate with your risk and need profile.

Simple

- Having optimal simple estate planning techniques in place to minimize estate taxation exposure to the fullest extent allowable by law.

Continuation

- Having an optimal continuation plan in place for your family and business(es).

Complex

- Further minimizing estate taxation exposure to the fullest extent allowable by law by identifying, comparing and implementing appropriate complex estate planning techniques that build upon the success of simple techniques.

Family

- Assisting adult children and adult grandchildren in career development, personal development and wealth mastery to the point of mitigating the risk of wealth depletion for generations.

Charity

- Enhancing your life and legacy and the lives of others with an optimal giving plan, structure, system, support and discipline.

Blue Print

- Having a simple yet comprehensive document that provides you, your spouse and, ultimately, your legal representatives and loved ones with a complete schematic of your financial position, trusted advisor team and estate plan.

Back-test/Stress-test (2 Strengths)

Back-test

- Having back-tested your financial security to every 40 year period going back to 1900 with a 4% or less probability of depletion, even under worst 10% of conditions.

Stress-test

- Having stress-tested your financial security under challenging circumstances and still passing the above back-test.

Wealth Optimization Makeover

Here is a simulated example of what a Wealth Optimization Makeover might look like for a high net worth investor with a portfolio of $1 million to $20 million. Notice how the 35 Essential Strengths™ turn from vulnerabilities and weaknesses to strengths in a relatively short period of time.

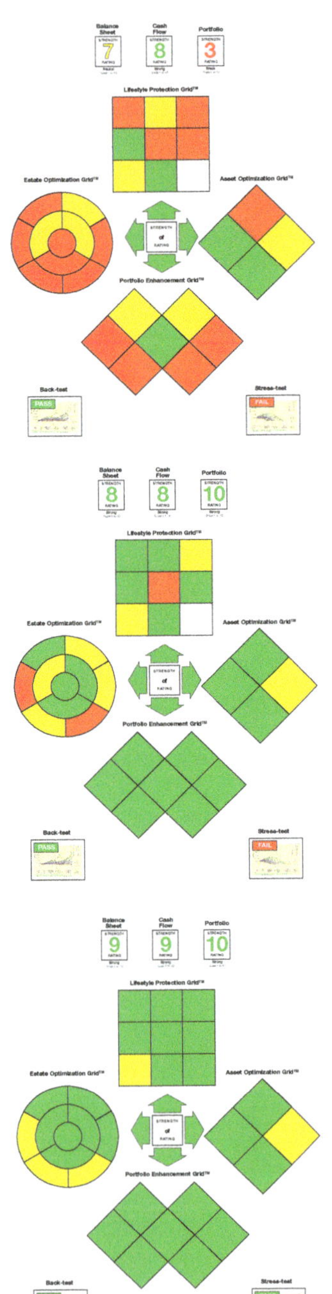

BEFORE

With less than one-third of the 35 Essential Strengths with a green (strength) rating, numerous issues (yellow) and big issues (red) are exposed, providing this investor with tremendous direction on eliminating vulnerabilities, weaknesses and complexities that have been holding them back.

AFTER (6 months)

This investor took the analysis seriously and was highly motivated to bring their finances to a new level of optimization. They brought two-thirds of the categories into the green (strength) zone in just six months. This provided an even more focused plan of improvement for the year ahead.

AFTER (3 years)

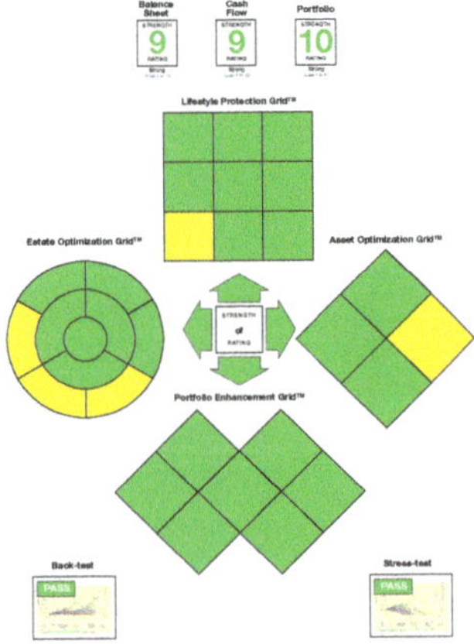

This investor realized that mastering money is not as difficult as it seems when they have the right structure, systems, support, and discipline in place. Just three-years into the process they have 90% of the categories in green (strength) zone and are chipping away at the others. They know they are in a good place and know that they are Investing from a Position of Strength.

"The little pig with the portfolio of straw and the little pig with the portfolio of sticks were swallowed up, but the little pig with the portfolio of bricks withstood the dip in the market."

from, and how many weaknesses you need to address. Achieving 30 or more of the 35 Essential Strengths can take three to 10 years in all, but that position, once achieved, is tantamount to complete financial freedom.

The opposite of structure is not disorder; it is paralysis. Investors who lack a wealth structure may be paralyzed by uncertainty or by an abundance of opportunities. They find it hard to move forward because it is unclear in which direction "forward" lies. The right structure dispels confusion. It spurs action by showing precisely where action is needed and what benefits will result.

I encourage you to read each of the 35 Essential Strengths in the bonus section. I bet they will strike you as attributes you would like to attain. For the purposes of this quick-read book, I have provided succinct, outcome-based definitions in lieu of lengthy, in-depth explanations. However, don't let my brevity belie the financial strength that results when all 35 strengths are achieved.

Peace of mind and clarity of purpose

When I take a client through the Five Guiding Principles (chapter 3) and the 35 Essential Strengths, something special happens. Recently, a couple, "Jill" and "Tom," went through this process. Not only did they realize that they could transition to retirement in the following year, which was their goal, they also learned they could spend more than they had been spending and still pass our stress tests with flying colors.

The surest way to get what you want is to deserve what you want.

CHARLEY MUNGER

To be a superior investor and achieve high-level financial security and independence, master the techniques of *Investing from a Position of Strength.* Avoid the incomplete approaches offered by value extracting brokerage, banking, insurance and mutual fund industries.

– Joseph J. Janiczek

At the end of the meeting, Tom choked up a bit and said, "Thank you. You gave me my wife back." I learned that before they became aware of my system and structure, Jill was spending most of her free time trying to stay on top of financial issues. Tom said the process we took them through freed her of these concerns, and they were now enjoying great time together. That alone was a huge practical advantage.

The right system and structure provide great peace of mind and clarity of purpose. They liberate investors from the day-to-day burden of focusing on their wealth, and they also put them in the proper psychological state to invest successfully.

Imagine knowing that you have 30 of the 35 Essential Strengths nailed. Imagine that you have passed extreme back-tests and stress tests. Would this provide you with the confidence to invest for the long run? Would it make you comfortable enough in bear markets to invest at deep discounts when others are overcome by fear? Would it help you to recognize bubbles and harvest profits before they burst, and not worry about what you may have left on the table? These are just some of the advantages of investing from a position of strength.

Do you feel ready now to design and build your own world-class wealth management structure? Probably not, nor would I recommend you try. Strong investors know their own talents and limits, so they don't go it alone. This brings me to the third pillar of financial strength: support.

Chapter Five

The Third Pillar: Support

Gaining Advantages and Avoiding Penalties

Abraham Lincoln's election occurred at a perilous juncture in American history. Some of his most important decisions were made the day after he learned he had become the nation's next leader. Lincoln later confided his initial response to learning he had won the presidency.

> *"I was there without leaving [at the Springfield, Illinois telegraph office], after the returns began to come in until we had enough to satisfy us as to how the election had gone. I went home, but not to get much sleep, for I felt then, as I never had before, the responsibility that was upon me. I began to feel at once that I needed support—others to share with me the burden. This was on Wednesday morning, and, before the sun went down, I had made up my cabinet. It was almost the same that I finally appointed."**

Historians still marvel at the remarkable nature of Lincoln's cabinet appointments. He did not reward friends or supporters, as is often the custom, and he didn't choose men who saw everything the way he did. Three of his eight choices, William Seward (Secretary of State), Salmon Chase (Secretary of the Treasury), and Edward Bates (Attorney General), had been rivals for the presidency and fierce critics of Lincoln. Edwin Stanton (Secretary of War) had treated him with contempt in their only previous meeting and later referred to him as a "long-armed ape." Lincoln did not care about past insults.

Lincoln had one goal that trumped every other consideration finding the talent he needed to cope with the looming crisis. He possessed the strength of character to overlook other concerns and a talent for recognizing other's talents.

Investors often are willing to settle for less than the best when seeking advice and support. They choose talent based on secondary factors that are not aligned with their own needs or interests. Some people let sentiment interfere with sound judgment by turning to friends or people they have met socially.

* From the Diary of Gideon Welles, published by Houghton Mifflin Co. of Boston in 1925.

Others allow themselves to be awed by the sheer size of the large Wall Street brokerage houses. As the financial crisis of 2008 and more recent developments have shown, size is not a reliable marker for talent or great support.

Do I need an advisor?

A fundamental question posed by many investors today is, "Do I actually need an advisor?" They may question the merits of working with an advisor for various reasons. If investors go it alone because it is their money and no one cares more about seeing it grow than they do, the result is a setup for misplaced self-confidence and undesirable outcomes.

The information age has made it much easier to fly solo, but it has not made it easier to succeed. You can make trades on your own over the Internet. You can get a ton of free information and advice. (Consider that it is free for a reason.) You may even do fairly well, for a while at least, through luck or the benefits of a bull market. However, with rare exceptions, do-it-yourself investors are just as successful as untrained do-it-yourself lawyers, doctors, architects, etc. Studies show that when taxes, fees, and other expenses are taken into account, about 80 percent of day traders lose money annually, and just one percent are consistently profitable. Worse is that people who go this route often end up neglecting their real talents, the ones that allowed them to generate wealth in the first place.

It is not that successful people lack the intelligence to invest wisely, but intelligence is not the only prerequisite. You need time, depth of knowledge, and experience that a quality advisor offers, and a sophisticated, expensive infrastructure. The tools, technology, information, and research required to do investing the right way are well beyond the means of a private investor. A successful advisor can spread these costs over hundreds of clients. A do-it-yourselfer cannot.

For these reasons, I consider support the third pillar of financial strength. It is required to build the system and structure and to access the right tools, the right trading platforms, and the best research. Your real challenge lies in identifying the talent and support required to become a strong investor.

Your search for support should always be based on objective standards of excellence. Clear standards will help you determine just what sort of talent you need, and reduce the risk of being swayed by personal appeals or corporate marketing. The standards do not have to be complicated or difficult to assess. In fact, you can learn an enormous amount by asking five simple questions:

"It's a funny thing about life; if you refuse to accept anything but the best, you very often get it."

SOMERSET MAUGHAN

Investors with seven- and eight-figure portfolios should endeavor to work with the very best and not settle for less. An action plan spurred on by this new vision of what is possible will usher in clear direction and inspire willing action.

– JOSEPH J. JANICZEK

- Is the advisor on your side and your side alone, or might he or she have other agendas or conflicts of interest?
- Does the advisor have a compensation structure aligned with your success?
- Does he or she provide clarity leading to confidence or confusion leading to dependence?
- Does the advisor have the expertise and do all the homework required to give sound advice?
- Can the advisor address all your financial needs or just a portion of your needs?

Is the advisor on your side and your side alone, or might he or she have other agendas or conflicts of interest?

In spring 2010, the Securities and Exchange Commission indicted Goldman Sachs on a charge of fraudulent misconduct stemming from the company's sale of securitized subprime home loans to its clients. The firm was accused of selling its clients an exotic investment vehicle known as a collateralized debt obligation (CDO*), while betting, simultaneously and accurately, that this same CDO they were selling would plunge in value. While Goldman neither admitted nor denied any wrongdoing, the bank later acknowledged it had made a "mistake" and had provided "incomplete information" to its clients. Goldman's settlement with the SEC included payment of a $300 million fine and $250 million in restitution to investors—the largest penalty ever levied by the SEC.

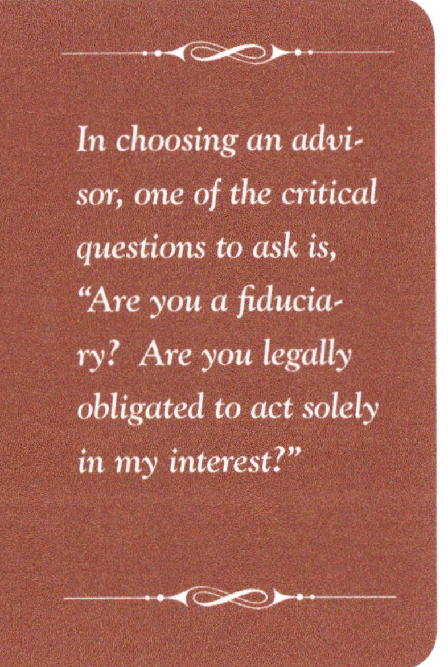

Goldman's actions amounted to an outrageous conflict of interest. They were profiting from their clients' misplaced trust when they made the initial sale of the CDO, and they profited even more from their clients' losses. What is even more outrageous is that such conflicts are normally viewed as perfectly legal, and Wall Street has lobbied heavily to ensure they remain legal. The industry has resisted attempts to be designated as fiduciaries, which would make them legally obligated to act in

collateralized debt obligation (CDO): a type of structured asset-backed security whose value and payments are derived from a portfolio of fixed-income underlying assets. CDOs securities are split into different risk classes, or tranches, whereby "senior" tranches are considered the safest securities. Interest and principal payments are made in order of seniority, so that junior tranches offer higher coupon payments (and interest rates) or lower prices to compensate for additional default risk.

"Being in possession of great wealth made me a bit self-conscious at first, but I finally came to terms with it."

their clients' best interests.

When choosing an advisor, one of the critical questions to ask is, "Are you a fiduciary?" That is, is the advisor legally obligated to act solely in your interest? If the answer is yes, you have a foundation of trust on which to build. If the answer is no, you may be dealing with someone with divided loyalties. Non-fiduciary advisors have a primary loyalty to their employer. This divided loyalty leads to practices that undermine clients' best interests. Most of the bad behavior described in this chapter is a result of this core problem.

Does the advisor have a compensation structure aligned with your success?

There is another layer of protection that many fiduciary advisors provide: They work on a fee-only basis. All advisors need to be compensated for their work, but fee-only advisors receive all their compensation from their clients. That means they have no financial stake in the products they recommend, unlike "fee-based" advisors and commission-based advisors, whose compensation may depend on pushing certain investments rather than others. I regard this practice as a serious conflict of interest and a justifiable source of mistrust. The scandal at Goldman Sachs is a recent, glaring example of a more subtle, pervasive problem. I have met scores of investors burned by dubious products that their one-time "advisors" had a personal reason to tout.

Not all advisors who receive commissions are dishonest or unethical. I know good, smart people who work on that basis. Even so, there is a problem. You are still at a significant disadvantage compared to the benefits you receive by working with a quality fee-only advisor. As the saying goes, "You get what you pay for," and if you do not have a fee-only advisor, you likely are paying for the wrong things. You may be paying substantial fees and other costs for the right to purchase your investments. Your payment may be buying you little more than access to securities at heavily marked up retail prices rather than getting value added services and using institutional or other lower cost versions of the same or similar vehicles offered by the retail broker or advisor.

Many investors do not realize these costs can be a total waste of money. They may not provide any value and likely are a penalty, pure and simple. In the long run, the size of the penalty is much larger than most investors realize. Just as the magic of compounding can turn small, regular savings into a large nest egg, it can also transform small annual costs into a major deficit over time.

For example, say you decide to make a long-term investment of $100,000 in the stock market, and you have two routes to consider.

- Fund A offers a well-diversified portfolio of stocks selected by the fund's managers. It has a cost ratio of 2.03% annually.
- Fund B is a non-managed market index fund, with a cost ratio of just .15% annually.

For the sake of comparison, let's assume that both funds perform equally well, with a gross annual return of 9%. What difference will the larger cost make to your long-term return on investment?

- After 10 years, Fund A will be worth $37,000 less due to its higher cost, with a value of $196,000, compared to $233,000 in Fund B.
- After 30 years, Fund A will have a value of $755,000, while Fund B will be worth $1.27 million. The managed fund's "reasonable" 2% annual cost adds up to half a million dollars more in long-term expenses!*

Investors should expect and demand cost-efficient investment vehicles. The options include bundles of stocks known as Exchange-Traded Funds

* Calculation originally made by David Ning at Moneyning.com (http://moneyning.com/investing/the-impact-of-costs-on-mutual-fund-returns/)

(ETFs), which have cost ratios as much as ten times lower than the typical mutual fund. Moreover, registered investment advisors, institutional investors, and large investors can gain access to securities, funds and vehicles of all types at preferred pricing and without the front-end or back-end fees that the average investor pays. If you work with an institution or advisor who passes these savings on to you, you can avoid the penalty of paying high, unnecessary fees. It is a no-brainer way to increase your portfolio performance.

A good fiduciary, fee-only advisor will bill clients 1% or less annually for investment management and wealth management services. But observe the distinction: Instead of paying this amount or more for a low-value service (merely purchasing investments), you're paying the same amount or less for a high-value service (impartial investment advice, portfolio management and the system, structure, support and discipline of wealth management). A low-value service is little more than a toll, and an unnecessary one at that. With a high-value service, you're purchasing the system, structure, support, and discipline needed to master wealth and become a strong investor.

Moreover, with a fee-only advisor, your interests are much better aligned. Fee-only advisors increase their own compensation by growing the wealth of the people they serve. By contrast, non-fiduciary, commission-based advisors often get a large hit of income the moment you make the transaction and then little or nothing. This is why you often do not hear from them until the next transaction. They do not have to add value to be successful. They just need to

"Feeling poorly? Thank heaven! I thought you said you were feeling poor."

look the part until you say yes. They just have to hook clients and keep them hooked, often by generating fog and complexity.

Does the advisor provide clarity leading to confidence or confusion leading to dependence?

To a certain extent, the financial crisis that broke in 2008 can be described as a case of Wall Street being hoisted by its own petard. Large brokerage houses often use complexity to create confusion and dependence, and to extract value rather than add value. In 2008, many large firms did the exact same thing to themselves. The exotic financial instruments that sparked the banking crisis were so arcane, no one could predict or control the damage once the dominoes started to fall. It is no wonder that Warren Buffett described derivatives as "financial weapons of mass destruction."

I have seen this same bewilderment on a much smaller scale among clients who are refugees from large firms. "Jane" is one of the more egregious examples. Jane's portfolio was a case of diversification run amuck. Jane had a $10 million portfolio, but you would never have guessed it by looking at a page torn from her list of investments. She had an incredible number of separate holdings and accounts, some with as little as $200 in one stock. Her monthly account statement looked like a phone book.

One of my services for new clients is a Portfolio Enhancement Plan, which includes two Portfolio Snapshots. The first illustrates the strengths and weaknesses of the present portfolio and the second shows the enhanced characteristics of an optimized and customized portfolio. In Jane's case, our initial challenge was inputting her current holdings into our portfolio analysis system. It took one of our staff members two and a half days to keystroke all the details. It was only then that Jane could finally see how poorly her total holdings had been performing. Her subpar returns had been completely obscured by a web of complexity woven by her former brokerage house.

This is not a rare occurrence among very high net worth individuals I see. It is a common strategy to chop a portfolio into small pieces because it generates work for the company—more accounting, more reporting, more commissions, etc. It also leaves the client feeling dependent, not self-confident, and it obscures costs and underperformance that might prompt clients to take their business elsewhere.

Quality advisors do just the opposite—they do not generate complexity, they cure it. They create easy-to-read account statements showing how your portfolio is performing. They give you the context behind the numbers by making it easy to compare your own investment returns with the market as a whole or the relevant peer groups. If they offer full-breadth advice, they make it easy to spot strengths and weaknesses. My wealth management reporting format, showcased in the bonus section, provides a one-page color-coded Wealth Optimization Dashboard™ that I utilize in providing clients with clarity. I do not expect my clients to have accounting backgrounds. I want them to be able to see at one glance where their attention is needed and where they are in great shape. I have a consolidated portfolio report that provides the clarity our clients need regarding their portfolio. It is prepared and available to our advisors and clients daily, not so clients can review theirs daily, but so the day they do they are looking at timely information.

Confusion is a sign that your advisor or broker is obscuring matters and keeping you off balance. Clarity is essential to becoming a strong investor, and if you do not have it now, demand it. In the short-term, newfound clarity can generate concern as you spot previously concealed problems. In the long-term, however, clarity leads to better decisions and greater confidence, not only in your advisor but in yourself.

Does the advisor have the expertise and do the homework required to give sound advice?

PricewaterhouseCoopers 2007 Global Private Banking/Wealth Management Survey says it all: "Wealth-management business CEOs rate only 17 percent of their current client relationship managers as having the skills to manage their clients." The 25-year multi-asset, mega bull market allowed the complete financial service profession to grow and prosper with borderline expertise at best. In fact, many "advisors" have great networking, golfing, and relationship skills and subpar investment and wealth management expertise. They look the part, so it is often difficult for a high net worth investor to see beyond the outside shell and discern tangible evidence of the needed expertise.

Talented people are both efficient and diligent. They do not waste effort by doing more than is necessary, and they do not spare effort by doing less than required to get great results. When it comes to investment advisors, the temptation to skimp on effort may be heightened because clients often cannot tell if they have done their homework or not. It is easy to create a portfolio that looks diversified but is not, or tout one as "customized" when, in fact, it consists of standard, off-the-shelf products. It is easy to say that they base their investment advice on careful research and keen foresight, when they are actually doing little research and basing recommendations on hindsight. These are common problems I see when I look at new clients' existing portfolios, and signs that their previous advisors were taking shortcuts.

The most common shortcut is rearview mirror investing. It is not unusual to see portfolios composed of last year's top funds or securities. This approach allows an advisor to 1) make quick, easy decisions, 2) to tell clients, "I've put you in all the top funds," and 3) to justify any failures that might occur ("Who could have possibly guessed Fund A would underperform the market?").

This approach is lazy and risky. Numerous studies show that there is no significant correlation between past success and future success in funds. The research suggests that the only safe bet is that bad funds tend to stay bad. Luck may indeed be fickle, but ineptitude won't desert you.

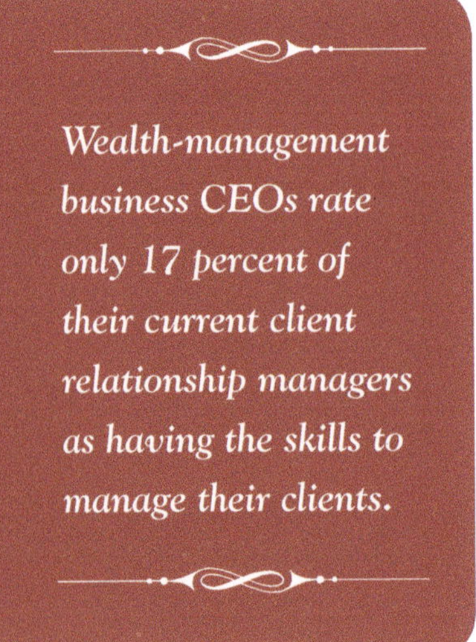

Does this observation mean that investing in funds is a total gamble? No, but it means that you have to evaluate securities with research that goes beyond a glance at past growth. The research required is not unlike the process that top fund managers use to select individual stocks. We use the "breadcrumb approach" at my company. We look for characteristics (advantages, systems, structures, talent, disciplines, and efficiencies) that in our judgment make the fund more likely to perform above average over the long haul.

A diligent advisor will also provide you with a truly diversified portfolio, not one that merely seems to be diversified. You may think you have achieved diversity because you have a long list of different holdings. However, if a preponderance of those holdings are in the same asset class, or the same sector, risk class, equity style, fixed income-style, or geographic location, you may be much more vulnerable than you realize. Holdings in these individual categories can sometimes move in unison, and if they move down, you will pay the price of having too many eggs in the wrong basket.

Diversification does not mean that the individual "eggs" are unimportant. Each should be picked as if the whole portfolio hinged on its success. Diversification can't become such a fetish that you fail to overweight some investments and underweight others for fear of upsetting some arbitrary notion of balance. Diversification is a way to hedge your assessments of future market performance. It is not a way to eliminate the need for prudent assessments and selection. Advisors with the right expertise will help you accomplish this important distinction.

Shortcuts cannot satisfy another legitimate need, customization.

Some large brokerage houses advertise that they offer portfolios tailored to the individual. What they really mean is they offer a range of off-the-shelf investments geared toward different ages and risk temperaments. These funds are no more "tailored," in the sense of customization, than the selection of suits available at any discount department store. Genuine customization means a willingness to adjust a client's portfolio to fit his or her unique circumstances and needs. Unlike a suit fitting, it is not a one-time event. As needs and situations change, a portfolio must be reviewed to ensure it is optimized in terms of risk, flexibility, and other key characteristics.

For example, clients of mine had a dream of buying an oceanfront home, and they had to be in a position to move very quickly when the right home came on the market. That required an adjustment to ensure they had sufficient liquid holdings that could be converted to cash, without the risk of huge swings in value, when they needed it. Ultimately, they were in a position to buy a spectacular piece of property at a distressed price while other potential buyers were distracted by volatile market moves.

Can the advisor address all your financial needs or just a portion of your needs?

This final question may be the most crucial one. One big mistake that most investors make in looking for talent is that they define the word "advisor" too narrowly. They focus on one component of their wealth, usually their investment portfolio, and they engage an advisor who only specializes in that area. The best approach is to think of advisors in three distinct forms: 1) those who provide investment advice only; 2) those who provide investment advice in combination with financial, retirement and estate planning (wealth management); and 3) those who provide investment advice in combination with financial, retirement, estate and legacy planning (multi-generational wealth management).

Investing from a position of strength is an approach that only advisors in alternatives two and three can provide. Despite the inherent pitfalls and potential dangers, I am amazed at how many high net worth investors go to an investment only shop. This choice is the source of many unaddressed needs and some of the poorest results I have observed.

I have also seen high net worth investors hire multiple investment-only advisors. They think they are diversifying risk when in fact overlap, inefficiencies, and other problems result from this approach. They are getting

Types of Advisors

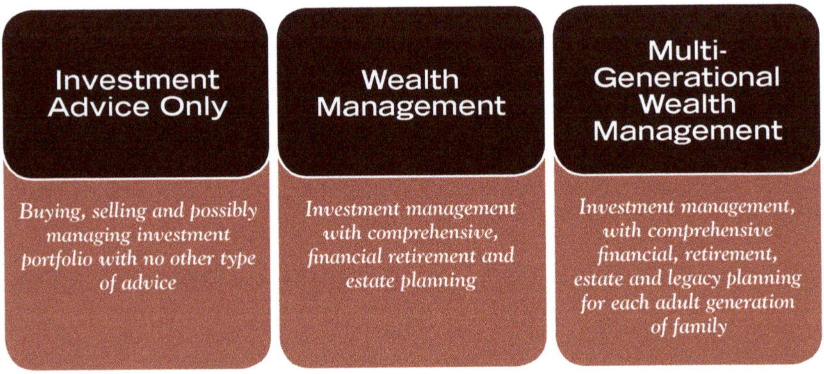

Investment Advice Only	Wealth Management	Multi-Generational Wealth Management
Buying, selling and possibly managing investment portfolio with no other type of advice	*Investment management with comprehensive, financial retirement and estate planning*	*Investment management, with comprehensive financial, retirement, estate and legacy planning for each adult generation of family*

a lot of advice trying to maintain accounts at multiple brokerages/advisors, but for all the advice they're receiving, they lack the most critical talent of all—a lead advisor. No one is helping them manage their wealth in a comprehensive manner.

One of the most popular products offered to high net worth investors by brokerages is Separate Account Manager accounts, or wrap-fee programs. Brokers like to assert that this is the sophisticated way to invest, that it is more tax savvy, and a bunch of other malarkey. At the same time, they insult mutual funds and ETFs and call them investment vehicles for small, unsophisticated investors. Clients who go this route wind up with complex statements that have so many holdings, they are impossible to decipher—an advantage to the broker, a huge disadvantage to the client. The idea is to persuade clients that investing is enormously complex, and that changing your approach, or your advisor, would be equally complicated. It is not. We unravel these complicated ways of owning the equivalent of a handful of expensive mutual funds all the time. This is just an expensive and complicated way of having multiple investment-only advisors.

Investment-only advisors rarely concern themselves with the shape of your balance sheet or cash flow. They do not offer clients advice on how to structure their assets, only their investments, and often just their equities. They can't see the opportunities or weaknesses lurking in your non-liquid or personal assets, and they can't tell you how best to protect your standard of living. You might have other advisors looking at some of these issues, but they have the same basic problem: Even if they are good at what they do, they can't see issues outside the arc of their specialty.

Consequently, if you lack a quality lead advisor, there will not be any one person, yourself included, who sees the big picture. You need this vantage point to build the system and structures necessary. Consequently, a good lead advisor needs to be a full-breadth advisor as well; otherwise he or she can't bring the perspective that is required to fill that role.

"'Wealth management' is grossly overused in the financial service industry. The vast majority of financial advisors—77.9% call themselves wealth managers. Yet just 8.4% truly fit this description." –Prince/Geraciotio

Many high net worth investors are not aware of the need for full-breadth advice, and they may not realize that such advice is available. The industry is dominated by investment-only advisors. Unfortunately it can be difficult to decipher what is what. Prince/Geraciotio studied 1,177 financial firms. In their study, they cited that "wealth management" is grossly overused in the financial service industry. The vast majority of financial advisors—77.9%—call themselves wealth managers. Yet just 8.4% truly fit this description!* Full-breadth advisors provide financial planning, retirement planning, and estate planning in addition to investment management services. The best ones, in my opinion, can provide superior investment advice because they can see your portfolio in the context of your overall position, not in isolation. For the same reason, they can provide genuine customization, and they can do wonders to protect your lifestyle aided by back-testing and stress-testing your complete financial situation—all necessary components of true financial strength.

There are also a handful of advisors, perhaps as few as one percent, who define "full-breadth" in a way that extends beyond the lives of the primary clients they serve. They provide intergenerational wealth management aimed at ensuring that wealth mastery is a part of the legacy clients leave behind. This is a major concern to many high net worth investors, and with good reason, because individuals fare much better at creating wealth than families fare at preserving it. Research shows that 70% of inherited wealth is depleted within one generation, and 95% is depleted within three generations.

I have seen a few people deal with this problem by leaving their estates to charity, and not because of estrangement from their heirs, but because they were genuinely concerned that the wealth would do more long-term harm

* Source: Wealth Management (Wealth Management Press, 2003); Prince & Associates, 2004. Analysis: CEG Worldwide, LLC

than good. If your goal is ensuring that your estate will truly benefit loved ones, there are other ways to accomplish this goal. I have developed programs that help family members learn to master wealth before they receive it, and to gain the perspective and skills they will need to manage wealth wisely and preserve it for their own heirs. See page 77 to learn more about this service offering.

There is a saying that it is harder to spot talent in others than it is to develop talent in yourself. That is why so many people reach a point of success that ends up becoming their ceiling. They reach the limit to which their talent can take them, and they won't, or can't, find additional talent to support their growth and success. That's why finding the right lead advisor is so essential.

If you identify a good, smart, trustworthy person to fill this role, I estimate that you have solved the bulk of your problems. You will get the structure, system, and support you need, and you will have a trusted ally in recruiting or retaining any other needed talent. Many of my clients had a good team in place before I met them, but the team lacked leadership. A team becomes more aligned and effective when one person is tasked with looking at the big picture. That is what a quality lead advisor provides.

At this point, I've covered nearly all that is needed to become truly financially strong. But strength in any arena of life requires one attribute I have yet to discuss. Some people have this in abundance while others struggle with it daily. Regardless, I believe I can help you acquire the discipline you need to master wealth.

Chapter Six
The Fourth Pillar: Discipline

The Strategic Exertion of Effort Where It Counts

You have to be intelligent to get into Mensa. They only accept applicants with IQs that place them in the top 2 percent of the population. One might expect that if Mensa members formed an investment club, their returns would exceed market averages, or at least match them. In actuality, between 1986 and 2001, while the S&P 500 was returning a robust 15.3% annually, the Mensa Investment Club had average returns of 2.5% per year.*

How did these geniuses and near geniuses manage such poor results in such a strong market? Their basic problem was a lack of discipline. Instead of using their intellects to determine a sound investment approach and sticking with it, they got sidetracked into exploring trendy new tools and theories of how to predict market trends. When one strategy didn't work they tried another. They made frequent trades, thus increasing their transaction costs. In short, they provided a perfect example of Warren Buffett's comment: "Investing is not a game where the guy with the 160 IQ beats the guy with the 130 IQ." Common sense and discipline will beat erratic genius every time.

I acknowledge that discipline may not be everyone's favorite word. For many of us, it is a reminder of all those things we ought to be doing but don't get around to. The word can leave us feeling partly guilty and partly annoyed. For others, the word prompts mental images of childhood mischievousness and consequences. For our discussion, becoming financially strong, the pertinent definition is "a method of practice; mastery."

In investing terms, discipline is not as harsh a taskmaster as it may be in other situations. If you want to lose weight, for example, you must adopt different eating and exercise habits. Sticking with that commitment demands a large share of your daily allotment of self-control. By contrast, financial strength demands less frequent and more strategic forms of exertion.

* Source: Eleanor Laise, "If We're So Smart, Why Aren't We Rich?" Dow Jones Newswire, May 15, 2001.

Moreover, you can delegate or automate a large chunk of the effort required.

It is important to apply discipline where and when it is needed. It is an indispensable attribute and the fourth pillar of financial strength. It complements and completes the first three pillars. The right system gives you automation and allows you to focus on the Essential 15%. The right structure gives you clarity, awareness, and control—a platform for comprehensive success. The right support gives you expertise, tools, and resources you cannot obtain on your own. The right discipline makes certain you follow a rigorous process to gain the most out of the system, structure, and support on an ongoing basis. The first three put you in the driver's seat. Discipline revs the engine, gets you started, and keeps you moving.

It is imperative that you have discipline, but by "you," I do not necessarily mean you personally. I mean you in the larger sense of your support team. The idea is to minimize the activities that demand your personal effort. We all have personal limitations in terms of our time, energy, and attention. The purpose of the first three pillars is to preserve these resources for the tasks that matter most and for the people and projects that truly excite us. Thus, we avoid unnecessarily wasting our valuable resources on secondary concerns and work that can be automated or delegated (the 85% Trap). It is the same with discipline. The lion's share of it can be outsourced.

Strength-Based Wealth Management

As I mentioned in Chapter 1, I pioneered and patented methods related to the discipline of Strength-Based Wealth Management (SBWM), which is all about empowering people to be accomplished, depletion-resistant stewards of wealth. This goes hand in hand with Evidence-Based Investing (EBI), a disciplined investment approach aimed at helping investors be accomplished, penalty-resistant investors. Our success formula is SBWM + EBI = Wealth Mastery, which encompasses the idea that with good financial behavior and rigorous, strength-based wealth management and evidence-based investing practices, the path is clear on how to master money. See page 71 for a graphic depicting this integration.

This system provides investors with three important disciplines automatically:

- The discipline of mastering the five Guiding Principles
- The discipline of mastering the 35 Essential Strengths

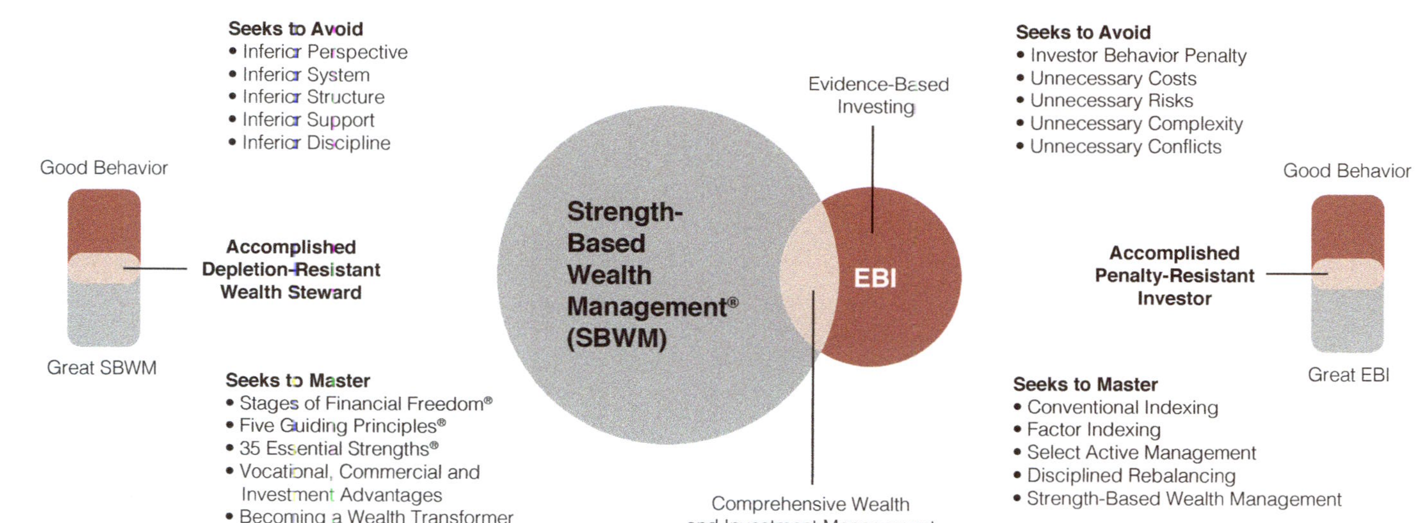
FORMULA FOR SUCCESS: SBWM + EBI = WEALTH MASTERY
Seeks to Avoid
• Inferior Perspective
• Inferior System
• Inferior Structure
• Inferior Support
• Inferior Discipline
Good Behavior
Great SBWM
Accomplished Depletion-Resistant Wealth Steward
Seeks to Master
• Stages of Financial Freedom®
• Five Guiding Principles®
• 35 Essential Strengths®
• Vocational, Commercial and Investment Advantages
• Becoming a Wealth Transformer
Strength-Based Wealth Management® (SBWM)
EBI
Evidence-Based Investing
Comprehensive Wealth and Investment Management
Seeks to Avoid
• Investor Behavior Penalty
• Unnecessary Costs
• Unnecessary Risks
• Unnecessary Complexity
• Unnecessary Conflicts
Good Behavior
Great EBI
Accomplished Penalty-Resistant Investor
Seeks to Master
• Conventional Indexing
• Factor Indexing
• Select Active Management
• Disciplined Rebalancing
• Strength-Based Wealth Management

- The discipline of mastering sound investment portfolio management, delegated to a professional lead advisor, which benefits by the huge advantage of investing from a position of strength.

The task of putting these disciplines into action falls primarily to your support team. Eighty-five percent of the discipline required to master wealth can be done on your behalf if you have a quality advisor leading you through a process like SBWM + EBI.

In my company, we offer a service level, the Complete Wealth Solution™, that provides investment advice coupled with comprehensive financial, retirement, and estate planning. At the beginning of an engagement and every two years thereafter, we take clients using this service through a Wealth Optimization Plan that achieves the first two disciplines cited above. At the same time, we provide a Portfolio Enhancement Plan to put the third discipline on automatic. This is what we mean by Wealth with Ease. The fee for this service may be the same or lower than the commissions or fees some brokers may charge for merely selling financial products.

"After my gall-bladder operation, I said to myself, 'Whoa, man, what are you doing with your life?' So I sold my blue chips, and put it all into Treasury bills."

Automation will take over integrated tools and it will make man obsolete as a specialist. Man will be forced back to what he was born to be—a comprehensivist—and to learn those generalized principles and to become master of his situation.

BUCKMINSTER FULLER

Amazing things happen when investors allow prudent wealth management automation to serve them. Huge space opens allowing focus on one's highest purpose, greatest abilities, and biggest opportunities—an ideal environment for personal breakthroughs, continued wealth creation, and maximum contribution to family, community, and world.

– Joseph J. Janiczek

Focus Your Personal Discipline Where it Counts—The High Five™

By automating or delegating a huge share of the discipline needed to master wealth, you can reserve your self-discipline for situations where it is needed most, making it a strategic asset, not an overdrawn account. This is one of the secrets of the successful people with whom I have the privilege to work. They devote their best to challenges associated with their greatest ambitions, rather than squandering valuable energy on secondary pursuits.

At this point in your journey toward financial strength, you already have great momentum. All you need to reach the goal line is to exercise self-control in a few vital areas. I call them the High Five because they are the key to achieving your highest potential in life. They are:

- Saving Awareness and Control Discipline
- Spending Awareness and Control Discipline
- Work Ethic Discipline
- Goal-Setting Discipline
- Learning Discipline

Saving discipline starts with figuring out what you need to save to reach your goals, and then treating that amount like any other bill you need to pay each month. Saving discipline is easily automated with direct deposits to a 401k or other investment accounts. Automating spending discipline will simplify that as well. The most common spending problem I see is not living beyond one's means, though that certainly happens. The more common problems are a lack of spending awareness and the excess time consumed by paying bills the old-fashioned way, which makes it harder to track where your money is going. With the tools I provide to my clients, it takes less than 30 minutes per month to manage expenses, and some clients have it down to 10 minutes. The same tools can generate reports to show if your spending is in line with your goals or not.

Work ethic discipline is not a matter of working hard, though that is part of it. It has much more to do with your strategy for deciding what to work on and what to delegate. It is easy to be pulled into handling tasks that you do very well, but if those activities do not energize you, they can be a dead end. It takes discipline to recognize this trap and ensure that your passions are not buried beneath your skills. You thrive when you are able to focus on activities for which you have endless energy, enthusiasm, opportunity, and talent.

That is where you want to direct your career and even your leisure pursuits, and that is also where goal-setting discipline comes into play. Goal setting turns the future into a resource. We need to have a vision of a future that is bigger than what we have been doing, even if we have been very successful up to that point. Among my clients, the ones who keep on growing and never plateau use goals as a powerful, inspirational resource. Goal setting generates energy and direction. Sometimes you succeed in reaching your goal, but even failures can bring surprise benefits if you are open to the value that can be extracted from nearly every experience.

By automating or delegating a huge share of the discipline needed to master wealth, you can save your own self-discipline for situations where it is needed most.

Using the past as a resource is a crucial aspect of learning discipline. The benefits of this discipline go well beyond the lessons it can provide. An outlook in life that is geared toward learning reduces fear and increases optimism. You do not want to be cavalier or blasé about failure, but you cannot let fear of failure curb your ambitions. By going into every new venture knowing that you will gain some useful insight along the way, you can keep a positive outlook that will enhance your long-term success.

These High Five disciplines can be mastered by anyone, and they all pay high dividends in the form of wealth creation and preservation. More importantly, they are essential to living a meaningful, productive, and fulfilling life. They reflect the capacity for self-control that distinguishes humans from other species. This same trait distinguishes strong investors from typical investors.

Putting the High Five to Work

I have seen the huge rewards that these disciplines bring for clients like "George," a successful executive, who had stock options valued at tens of millions of dollars when he decided to retire. His success in the business world derived from the passion he brought to his work, and when he retired, he rechanneled his work ethic discipline in new directions. George and his wife, Shelly, set a new goal to make the world a better place and help children in particular. Toward that end, George and Shelly used half of their wealth to establish their own charitable foundation, putting their enthusiasm and talent into the task of identifying the best charities to support. Because they had put their wealth on automatic, George and Shelly could devote themselves to this new and fulfilling mission. Their wealth was not a problem to manage or a distraction from the things that mattered most to them. It was a strength.

Another client, "David," came to me in the prime of his career. He had amassed a portfolio of about $5 million—more than enough to maintain his desired standard of living for the rest of his and his wife's lifetime—and we gave him the system, support, structure, and discipline to achieve that. This security gave David the freedom to explore a new direction in his career. He became CEO of a billion-dollar company with thousands of employees. By having his wealth on automatic and focusing on the High Five disciplines—the work ethic, the goal setting, the learning discipline, and still controlling his saving and his spending—he was able to more than double his net worth by the time he was ready to consider retirement. He is now in a great position to transition to the next phase of his life, which may include more of a focus on leisure and charitable activities.

For other clients, financial freedom opens the door to a long-postponed ambition. One couple, "Tim and Jennifer," shared a love for the visual arts, but the daily demands of two successful careers did not leave time to pursue that hobby. After seeing that they could master the spending and saving disciplines and live comfortably within their means, they set a new goal to follow the dream they had looked forward to throughout their marriage. They sold their home and moved to a creative community, with a culture that matched their love for the outdoors and the visual arts. They are truly enjoying the leisure and benefits of the wealth they created together.

What Are Your Own Possibilities?

Sometimes, the pursuit of wealth can leave a void in our lives—a place left empty because we lacked the energy or time to pursue a dream. There is a saying: "Wealth is not an end, it is a means to an end." The problem is that the complexity of creating and managing wealth often gets in the way of seeing and pursuing an end truly aligned with your highest purpose in life.

My life's work has been focused on this critical unmet need. I hope this book has helped you to see the possibilities that open up once you escape from the chaos and confusion that characterize so much of the wealth management field today. I absolutely know it is possible to put a large portion of wealth management on automatic; I have built the system, structure, support and discipline to achieve this; and I've seen how using these benefits helps people define and achieve their highest ambitions. This approach is both effective and rewarding.

Clients are surprised sometimes when I ask them about their higher purpose and possibilities. It is not that they feel I'm prying; they just don't expect an advisor to be concerned with such matters. I tell them that these are the most important questions for them to consider.

On the practical side, wealth needs a purpose the way a compass needs a magnetic field. The whole enterprise of managing wealth must be pointed in some direction and have a goal that inspires and justifies the effort. If there is no goal or the goal is not inspiring, it is hard to summon the energy and commitment that wealth mastery requires. Also, I find that by opening up the horizon of higher purpose, clients become more eager to hand over tasks that are easy to automate and delegate. When any of us hit a ceiling, one powerful technique for breaking through the ceiling is to figure out what can be let go. The better you get at defining and pursuing your higher purpose, the more you can see that wealth management is something that needs to be done, but not by you.

Beyond these practical concerns, there is still the much larger, more vital question of purpose. Since wealth is a means to an end, that end lies elsewhere. The journey to master wealth should begin with this higher end sharply in focus.

"And I happen to know they won't let you take them with you down there, either."

A friend of mine, who has a Ph.D. in philosophy, notes that there is a very large distinction between "freedom from" and "freedom for." Sometimes, when I hear people discuss what financial freedom means to them, it is clear they're thinking primarily in terms of freedom from.

They would like to be free from anxiety over money, free from reliance on others for their income or security, and free from any type of work they find tedious or stressful. These are perfectly understandable, reasonable and achievable desires, but the greater value of wealth lies in freedom *for*, not freedom *from*. Discovering what you stand for and what you are working for is essential in life. It is equally essential in wealth management.

What is your highest purpose in life? Can you think of five regrets you would not want to have with you at the end of your life? What can you begin doing today, and every day going forward, to erase these potential regrets and turn them into sources of great satisfaction? This is one of many ways to get in touch with what is most important to you.

What haven't you done that you have always wanted to do, and still can do if you set your mind to it? Are there experiences, hobbies, activities, or causes that interest you? These may be rich areas of personal, intellectual, or spiritual growth that you can pursue now or in the near future.

Many experts on happiness say that the deepest and most enduring fulfillment comes from making meaningful contributions to others. Who are the most important people in your life, in your community, and in the world as you see it? What contributions would make you feel that the world is a better place for your having lived?

My purpose in life is helping other people to reach their potential by making wealth a source of strength and peace of mind. It is my privilege and pleasure to work each day with highly successful people, and to complement their existing strengths with my own expertise and the wonderful team and organization I have assembled. I love the "Ah ha!" moment people have when they get a clearer look at their finances than they have ever seen before. I love the smiles and satisfaction they share when they see old weaknesses turned into strengths. The thing I love most is helping people reach a new level, as their growing strength allows them to spread their wings and take off in new and exciting directions. My aim is to do this for every client, and, if given the opportunity, for every client's family to make financial strength an enduring gift and legacy.

MOVING FORWARD

A one-on-one personal consultation with one of our advisors in person at our headquarters, via phone, or via Internet.

If you are qualified ($1.5 million in investable assets or more), and would like a complimentary consultation with one of our advisors, see our website at www.janiczek.com. We are happy to review your situation, goals, and portfolio, and provide you with an expert recommendation as to appropriate next steps. Our advisor will also assess your needs and provide a recommendation as to what service package may fit you best—if you are interested in considering a professional working relationship with our firm. Our aim is to be a valuable resource no matter what. You may also reach us at 303-721-7000 or info@janiczek.com.

About Janiczek Wealth Management

About Janiczek Wealth Management

Accepting clients throughout the U.S., Janiczek Wealth Management offers comprehensive wealth management services to individuals and families with investable assets of $1.5 million and more. Specifically, we serve high net worth investors (with portfolios of $1.5 million to $20 million) and ultra-high net worth investors (with portfolios of $20+ million.)

When you put your assets in the hands of Janiczek Wealth Management, you are gaining insight and expertise recognized throughout the wealth management industry. We wrote the award-winning book *How to Achieve Absolute Financial Freedom*, the ground-breaking book, *Investing from a Position of Strength*, and more recently *Family Wealth*. We have been named among the top, best, and most exclusive advisors in the nation multiple times. Joseph J. Janiczek, our founder, was singled out as one of "Three Masters of the Retirement Universe" (along with Charles Schwab and economist Lawrence Lindsey) for his unique insights on attaining financial strength and independence. (Please see **Important Disclosure Information** on page 86.)

Today, decades after our founding, Janiczek Wealth Management is a full service, highly experienced team of professionals, who combine an in-depth knowledge of wealth management with a commitment to caring service. Our in-house experts in investment management and financial, retirement, tax and estate planning can work with your own trusted advisors (accountant, attorney, etc.) to provide you with complete, well-balanced support.

About our Unique Investor-Advisor Approach

The core of a great investor-advisor relationship is trust. At Janiczek Wealth Management we strive to earn your trust every day by building our relationship with you on four commitments:

- We provide you with the security of a **fiduciary** relationship. That means we are legally obligated to provide you with advice that is in your best interest, not our own interest or anyone else's.
- We are a **fee-only** advisor. The key word here is *only*. We receive no outside compensation for anything we do on your behalf. Unlike "fee-based" advisors or commissioned brokers, who represent companies and products, we have no divided loyalties.
- We practice **full disclosure**. We have no secrets or hidden agendas that might represent a potential conflict of interest.
- Since trust is based not only on integrity but on competence, we provide the advantages of a **full-breadth** advisor. From investment management to financial, retirement, and estate planning, we can manage all of your needs, detecting and addressing potential obstacles before they turn into problems.

About Our Service Package Menu

We recommend one of three service package solutions depending upon the scope of your needs and objectives. Over the years, we have found that high net worth investors have needs in three distinct groups and the most common of these is our Complete Wealth Solution. A review with one of our advisors will assist in pin-pointing the service package that is best aligned with your needs, circumstances and objectives.

The Complete Wealth Solution™
Investing with Strength, Systems, Structure, Support and Discipline
Our Complete Wealth Solution is our flagship service package. This service solution is the basis for this book. The Five Guiding Principles, 35 Essential Strengths, and the system, structure, support and discipline to help master them are all a part of this service. Think of it as a comprehensive investment management service integrated with our best financial, retirement, and estate planning optimization techniques.

The Complete Legacy Solution™
Investing with Strength, System, Structure, Support and Discipline... for Generations
If your goal is to master all the elements of the Complete Wealth Solution for yourself and you would like your adult children and perhaps adult grandchildren to master money, this service package is for you. It includes all the services of the Complete Wealth Solution for you plus annual family meetings and coaching and advising of adult children and grandchildren. It is an ideal way to make money mastery a part of your legacy and prepare family members for a potentially large inheritance.

The Complete Investment Solution™
Investing with System, Structure, Support and Discipline
This service package is an investment management only service designed for situations in which integrated financial, retirement and estate planning (to build financial strength) are not needed, such as when investing assets in qualified retirement plan trusts, charitable trusts, foundations or funds in other entities that are not tied to one individual or couple. It includes the robust investment management components of our services but none of the financial, retirement or estate planning optimization techniques.

The above is a summary of our services. Please contact us for further details and be sure to read our ADV Part II disclosure document before selecting a particular service package. Our advisors will be happy to review your circumstances, needs, and objectives and recommend the appropriate package before a final selection is made. (Please see **Important Disclosure Information** page that follows.)

Please contact us at 303-721-7000 or email us at info@janiczek.com. We will further introduce you to our company and arrange for you to discuss your needs and objectives with one of our advisors.

We offer those high net worth investors meeting our client standards a complimentary Discovery Session and/or Portfolio Review Session to pinpoint your needs and objectives and to receive a specific proposal of services recommended.

Contact Information

Janiczek Wealth Management
7001 E. Belleview Ave., Suite 600
Denver, CO 80237
303-721-7000
www.janiczek.com
info@janiczek.com

Important Disclosure Information

Past performance may not be indicative of future results. Different types of investments involve varying degrees of risk. Therefore, it should not be assumed that future performance of any specific investment or investment strategy (including the investments and/or investment strategies recommended and/or undertaken by Janiczek Wealth Management, Ltd. ("Janiczek"), or any non-investment related services, will be profitable, equal any historical performance level(s), be suitable for your portfolio or individual situation, or prove successful. Janiczek is neither a law firm nor accounting firm, and no portion of its services should be construed as legal or accounting advice. Moreover, you should not assume that any discussion or information contained in this document serves as the receipt of, or as a substitute for, personalized investment advice from Janiczek. Please remember that it remains your responsibility to advise Janiczek, in writing, if there are any changes in your personal/financial situation or investment objectives for the purpose of reviewing/evaluating/revising our previous recommendations and/or services, or if you would like to impose, add, or to modify any reasonable restrictions to our investment advisory services. A copy of our current written disclosure Brochure discussing our advisory services and fees is available upon request. The scope of the services to be provided depends upon the needs of the client and the terms of the engagement.

Sources: Barron's March 2017, 2016, 2015, 2014; AdvisoryHQ March 2018, 2017, 2016; Financial Times June 2017, 2015; Five Star Professional November 2016, 2015, 2014, 2013; Mutual Funds Magazine January 2001; NABCAP September 2013, 2011, 2010; Worth Magazine October 2008, October 2004, January 2004, July 2002; Wealth & Finance International October 2014.

Please Note: Rankings and/or recognition by unaffiliated rating services and/or publications should not be construed by a client or prospective client as a guarantee that he/she will experience a certain level of results if Janiczek is engaged, or continues to be engaged, to provide investment advisory services, nor should it be construed as a current or past endorsement of Janiczek by any of its clients. Rankings published by magazines, and others, generally base their selections exclusively on information prepared and/or submitted by the recognized adviser. Rankings are generally limited to participating advisers.

INDEX

ACKNOWLEDGMENTS

I thank all those clients, associates and peers, who, over the last 30 years, have helped us develop, refine and optimize all of the features of Strength-Based Wealth Management® and Evidence-Based Investing. In particular, John Keenan, Cindy DePuy, Linda Moore, Margie Hannum, and Monty Jorgensen provided invaluable advice and assistance in creating this book. I also thank Paul Winkler, Pam Dorn, Carole McKeown, Jim Callahan, CFA, Kyle Kersting, CFA, and Brady Siegrist for many years of persistent collaboration in getting to the Essential 15% of investment and wealth management and automating the system, structure, support and discipline outlined in this book.

Additionally, I thank my children, Margie Hannum and John Janiczek, and wife, Mary Janiczek, who greatly improved the book with their edits. Any errors or oversights, however, are solely mine.

Finally, I owe a debt of gratitude to all of the great thinkers quoted in this book who have helped me learn various concepts and wisdom from diverse industries so that I may apply them in the investment and wealth management fields. If they were not generous enough to share their learning with the world, it would have been difficult, if not impossible, to organize the strategies and techniques in this book into an actionable format.

Joseph J. Janiczek
February 2018

NOTES

NOTES

NOTES

NOTES

NOTES

NOTES

Investing from a Position of Strength

Personalize your experience! Enjoy any of six formats in any order.
Go to janiczek.com/strength for links to all.

READ THE BOOK	The book is designed to be read in an evening or during a short flight. Each of the six chapters explores one core concept, and simple chapter and subsection headings organize key need-to-know aspects of that chapter's core concept. **Estimated time: 1 hour**
GET THE PICTURE?	A picture is worth a thousand words, as are the illustrations throughout the book. A quick 15-minute review of these pictures and captions will provide a complete overview of the six core concepts. **Estimated time: 15 minutes**
LISTEN UP	The audio recording features a conversation during which the author answers questions about each core concept, elaborating on them in ways that will deepen your understanding. Listen to the audio at janiczek.com/strength. **Estimated time: 2 hours**
WATCH THIS	Consider learning or reviewing core concepts by watching a video synopsis. Watch the video at janiczek.com/strength. **Estimated time: 1 hour**
WHAT'S MY SCORE?	Use a scorecard to assess your current alignment with core concepts. Then, think ahead one year. What would you like your assessment to look like? Download the scorecard at janiczek.com/strength. **Estimated time: 10 minutes**
SHARE IT NOW	Instantly share a digital copy of the book with family, friends and colleagues at no cost! This is a powerful way to demonstrate your commitment to the concepts and begin conversations that can enhance your understanding and results. Go to janiczek.com/strength to share as many digital copies as you'd like, or, if you prefer to send books, you may order them using the same link. **Estimated time: 2 minutes or less**

www.ingramcontent.com/pod-product-compliance
Lightning Source LLC
Jackson TN
JSHW041740170426
101040JS00026B/567
9781948484053